P. A. Stuart

The Inside Guide To

Building Your Own Gaming Computer

1st Edition

Published by Lionhouse Publishing

ISBN-13: 978-1-999928575

Contents

Graphics Systems

Power Supply

Cases

Drives

Monitors

Assembling the Computer

Getting the System Operational

Peripherals

Overclocking

Troubleshooting

Gaming Resources

CHAPTER 1

First Things First

Introduction

Building a computer involves three stages - choosing the parts, assembling them and then setting up the system. In this opening chapter, we are going to concentrate on the former to make sure your parts will co-exist happily and provide you with a trouble-free gaming machine for some years to come.

The picture above shows a completed gaming computer. While putting it together is relatively straightforward, making sure you have used the *correct* components is much less so. This is actually the most difficult part of the job and involves a number of factors, all of which need to be carefully considered to ensure the finished PC not only works but is capable of doing what you intended it to.

A good example of this is the CPU, which connects to the motherboard via a socket. Processors from the two main manufacturers, Intel and AMD, use different types of socket so it is essential that the motherboard has the right one for the CPU you intend to buy. In the same vein, CPU sockets evolve as do the CPU's that connect to them, so don't assume that because you have opted for an Intel CPU it will fit into any Intel-based motherboard - it may not.

Something else to beware of is that you don't spend more than you need to and end up with a computer that has a processing power your games won't be able to utilise. They don't all require a hugely powerful computer!

So, to make sure you get it right from the start, we explain everything you need to know when buying each component. Chapters 2 to 9 investigate all the relevant specifications and features.

That done, we move on to the assembly stage in Chapter 10. Pictures and step-by-step instructions demonstrate the procedure as clearly as possible and ensure you don't make any mistakes. Many self-builders find this stage somewhat nerve-racking but it really is quite straightforward as you'll see.

Finally, the completed system will need to be set up. Pressing the power button for the first time will be the moment of truth when you find out if your new computer works. Assuming it does, you may then need to alter settings in the BIOS, install the operating system and get your hardware devices in tune with the operating system by downloading and installing the latest drivers. Chapter 11 gives you the low-down.

As speed and performance are prerequisites of a gaming computer, we have included a section on the subject of overclocking in Chapter 12. This is a method of getting certain components, namely the CPU, memory and graphics card, to run at higher speeds than they were designed to, with the intention of enhancing overall system performance.

Peripheral devices, such as the mouse, keyboard and game controllers, are essential elements of a gaming system and Chapter 13 takes a close look at what the gamer will require with respect to these devices.

Many self-builders encounter problems either because they've made a mistake somewhere along the way, or simply don't know what needs to be done, and in what order. A common issue here is neglecting to install device drivers. The computer may be running with everything appearing to be fine but, underneath the hood, without those drivers it will be spluttering along rather than roaring as it should be. Another is connecting the power button to the wrong pins on the motherboard, which of course means the computer won't switch on. To help resolve these issues, and others, a detailed troubleshooting guide is provided in Chapter 14. Hopefully, you won't need to refer to it.

We end with a look at some resources very popular with the gaming fraternity in Chapter 15. For example, sites such as Steam and GameSpot are used by millions of gamers around the world for news, reviews, trailers, forums and more. If you fancy having a go at game streaming, you'll be interested in OBS Studio; a free application that provides everything you need to get your games online. Then there's Hamachi, which lets you create safe virtual networks on which to play your games. There's plenty more here as well.

Pros & Cons of a Self-Built Computer

Before you get carried away at the prospect of building your own gaming PC, take a moment to consider the pros and cons. If it works, great - you'll have the satisifaction that comes with a successful outcome, not to mention a computer built to your exact specification. But what if it doesn't? It could end up being a very expensive mistake!

So, lets look at some very good reasons to simply buy it from a store:

Time & Effort

All you have to do is walk into your chosen store, pick the PC you want and then take it home. You could be using it within an hour or two, literally. Building it yourself, on the other hand, will take much longer - several days, probably. Sourcing the components will be a time-consuming process, particularly if you're buying online as you probably will be. Not only do you have to study component specifications, you have to wait for them to be delivered.

Then you have to build the thing. The actual assembling of the computer shouldn't take more than a couple of hours or so but you will also have to install the operating system, device drivers and your applications. This all takes time.

Aggravation

If it works, you won't have any. But if it doesn't, you will then have to find out what's gone wrong. It may be that you have damaged a component during the assembly stage. Or, you may have been unlucky enough to buy a faulty component (although rare, it does happen). In either case, you will have to get a replacement, possibly at extra cost and certainly more time.

If you can't establish what's wrong with the computer, you may have to take it to a repair store to get it fixed - again, more cost and time wasted.

Peace of Mind

A computer bought from a store will come with a guarantee. If you have any problems with it, just take it back for a refund or replacement. If you build it yourself, you're on your own when it goes wrong.

However, if you are prepared to ignore the potential pitfalls, there are some compelling reasons to go the DIY route. These include:

Hard Cash

Assuming you take the time to shop around for the best deals, building a computer yourself should cost less than buying the ready-made equivalent. The amount saved probably won't be that much, however, as PC's from the big manufacturers are keenly priced.

Quality

Many computer manufacturers cut costs by using low quality components. On paper, the specifications of a given computer may be impressive - the latest CPU, 8 GB of memory and a 1 TB hard drive, for example. But the drive may be an outdated mechanical model rather than the much faster SSDs now being used. The monitor might be a low resolution affair with a lifeless picture, while the power supply unit may be a cheap "made in China" device that's liable to burn out at any time.

Unless you have the knowledge to be able to look beyond the headline figures in the manufacturers specifications, they can be very deceptive. Building the PC yourself lets you choose good quality parts that will give you a reliable and long-lasting computer tailored to your exact requirements.

Future-Proofing

Most pre-built computers these days are all-in-one devices that cannot be opened up - Apple Macs are typical examples. This means they cannot be upgraded as and when newer and more advanced components become available. Because of this, given the speed at which computer technology is advancing, it's not long before they are obsolete.

A self-built computer, on the other hand, can be. You may have no need for a super-fast hard drive at the time of your build but by ensuring your motherboard can accept one of the latest NVME SSD drives, you can install one at a later date should it become necessary.

Software

All store-bought computers come with the operating system pre-installed which is fine. Unfortunately, many also come with less desirable software. We're talking here about what's known as "adware", which opens pop-up windows urging the user to download and install programs of various types. Anti-virus software is a typical example of this. There will probably also be time-limited software that works for a short period before needing to be paid for - Microsoft Office 365 for example. The term for this type of program is "bloatware".

These programs can be very difficult to get rid of. Building the PC yourself means you won't have this problem.

Guarantees

While a self-built computer may not come with a guarantee, each of the components inside it will. Although not as comprehensive as a manufacturer's system-wide guarantee, these will at least enable you to replace a faulty component at no cost.

What Do You Need It To Do?

Gaming isn't all about playing the latest resource-hungry games with all "guns blazing". While this does apply to a hardcore of gamers who will need a high-performance machine to get the best out of their games, for the majority who play less demanding games, the hardware requirements are much less.

In general, there are three types of gamer, each of whom have different requirements with regard to the power of their gaming machine.

The Professional Gamer

Professional gamers are those who play video games at a competitive level. For many, it's a full-time career and they are usually sponsored to compete in esports tournaments where large cash rewards are on offer. On a lower level are the players for whom video games are, at the very least, a serious hobby. For both, the demands of the games they play require a powerful computer. The components of a typical example are:

* CPU - Intel Core i9-10900K, 3.7 Ghz, Comet Lake
* Motherboard - Asus ROG MAXIMUS XII HERO
* Memory - Corsair Vengeance RGB PRO, 3000 Mhz, DDR4, 16 GB
* Graphics Card - NVIDIA GeForce RTX 2060 SUPER, 8 GB
* Drive - Samsung 970 EVO PLUS M.2 SSD, 1 TB
* Power Supply Unit - Corsair RMx 850 W
* Case - Fractal Design Define R6
* Monitor - Acer Predator XN253QXbmiprzx 24.5 inch FHD

At the time of writing, these parts cost £2500. Serious cash but the gamer will have a rig capable of not only playing all current games at the highest settings but also those to come in the forseeable future.

The Casual Gamer

The casual gamer is one who is relaxed about his/her gaming. It's not a full-time occupation and they are not as obsessive about it as the pro gamers. They play only when in the mood and restrict themselves in the main to low-level games, some of which don't actually need a gaming PC at all.

However, if they play mid-level games such as Grand Theft Auto, Far Cry, etc, they will need a bit more in the power stakes. A PC suitable for these gamers will look something like this:

* CPU - Intel Core i5-10600, 4.1 GHz, Comet Lake
* Motherboard - Asus PRIME Z490-P
* Memory - Corsair Vengeance LPX, 2666 MHz, DDR4, 8 GB
* Graphics Card - NVIDIA GeForce GT 1030, 2 GB
* Drive - Samsung 860 EVO SATA, 500 GB

...cont'd

- Power Supply Unit - Corsair CV450, CV Series, 450 W
- Case - MSI MAG VAMPIRIC 010
- Monitor - Samsung S24H650GDU 24 inch PLS

A computer of this specification currently costs £1000. While it bears no comparison to our pro model, it is still a powerful machine and will play the vast majority of games comfortably, although some settings may have to be turned down in the more demanding ones.

The Streaming Gamer

The live streaming of games is an activity where people record themselves playing games and stream them to an online audience. Currently, this is extremely popular and well known streaming platforms include Twitch, YouTube Gaming and Mixer.

Games like Fortnite, Call of Duty, Valorant and League of Legends are currently all the rage and they require some serious hardware in order to put on a good show. If this is an activity you intend to pursue, you will need a computer with components similar to these:

- CPU - Intel i5 10600K, 4.1 Ghz, Comet Lake
- Motherboard - Asus PRIME Z490-A
- Memory - Corsair Vengeance LPX 3000MHz, 8 GB
- Graphics Card - NVIDIA GeForce GTX 1660 - 6 GB,
- Hard Drive - Samsung 860 EVO SATA, 500 GB
- Power Supply Unit - GameMax 750W
- Case - Corsair Carbide SPEC 04
- Monitor - Acer XF240Hbmjdpr 24 inch, FHD, TN

This machine will set you back around £1300 and can be considered to be a mid-range gaming computer.

Please note that in the three setups we have described, most of the components chosen are the latest versions. So, economies can be made with little loss in performance if you go for slightly older models. For example, a 9th generation Core i5 CPU rather than a 10th generation Core i5.

Making Sure It Will Work

In the introduction to this chapter, we stressed the importance of your parts being compatible. As an example, we pointed out that the motherboard needs to have the right socket for the CPU. Other examples include the system case being large enough to take the parts, the power supply unit having the necessary wattage to power the system, and the memory (RAM) being supported by the motherboard.

There are two ways of ensuring this - the hard way and the easy way. The hard (and lengthy) way is to trawl through the specifications for each component, while the easy way is to let someone else do it for you.

To this end, all you need do is visit one of the many online system building configurators. These offer compatible options for every component in a computer. An example is shown below:

Start by selecting the CPU you intend to use.

...cont'd

Then go the motherboard section and you will be offered a list of compatible boards from the drop-down menu as we see here:

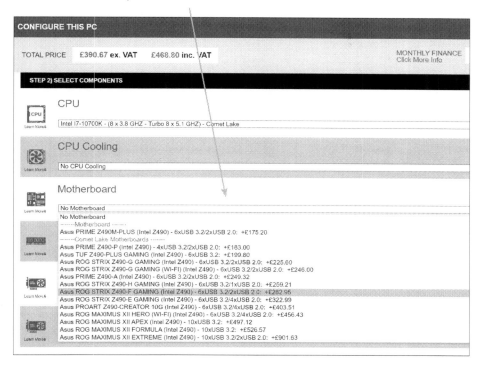

Working your way through the relevant sections will let you pick all the parts you need, safe in the knowledge they will be compatible. As you're doing so, you can keep an eye on how much you're spending in the Total Price section at the top of the page.

When you've finished, you'll be given a list of the selected parts. One thing to be aware of here is that some of these online configurators can be somewhat out of date, offering components that are not the latest. Also, some don't offer much in the way of choice. Our advice is to take a look at several before making any firm decisions, and to check the parts you're interested in aren't older versions.

Finally, just use these sites to draw up your list of components. Don't buy anything from them as you'll get better prices elsewhere.

Purchasing the Components

When it comes to actually purchasing your parts, you have two ways to go. The first is a computer store and the second is the Internet. These days, stores that sell individual computer parts are few and far between and, even if you can find one, this is where you'll pay the highest prices. That said, they do offer the advantage of convenience.

So for the vast majority of people, the Internet is the place to go. Prices online will be lower than anywhere else, plus you have access to an unparalelled amount of information about the products you are buying.

All the major computer manufacturers have an online presence, as do all the component manufacturers. Their online prices will almost always be lower than in the retail outlets.

The savvy shopper also has access to price comparison sites such as www. pricerunner.com in the UK and www.best-price.com in the USA. All you have to do is enter the product's details and you will be presented with a list of websites that sell the product together with the price.

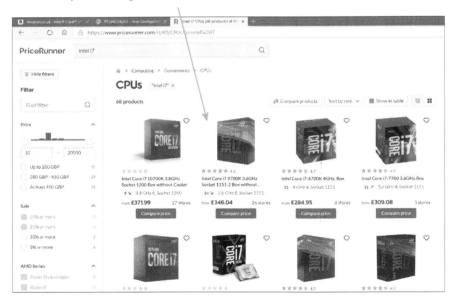

And if they're not enough, there's the now ubiquitous Amazon. Needless to say, the online behemoth sells computer parts along with just about everything else. What's more, you'll struggle to find any website that sells computer parts for less. An added bonus, and one well worth having, is Amazon's excellent returns policy. If you're not happy with a part for whatever reason, simply return it for a rapid, no-questions asked, refund.

...cont'd

When buying online, it will be as well to be aware of something known as OEM. This is an acronym for "Original Equipment Manufacturer" and is a term applicable to a company that manufactures products to be sold by a different company under their brand name.

Usually, these products are sold "barebones" without packaging, documentation, cables, manuals or bundled software. OEM products will also have a shorter guarantee and limited support. As a result, they cost less than the retail versions.

Mostly, they are sold to computer manufacturers in bulk. However, some do find their way on to the open market, online in particular where packaging isn't necessary to display and sell a product.

Because of the lack of packaging, registration cards, etc, there is a greater chance of getting a counterfeit product when buying OEM computer parts. It also has to be said that any savings are not likely to amount to much. Furthermore, if the device needs a cable, you may have to get one somewhere else.

All-in-all then, our recommendation is to give OEM parts a wide berth and pay the extra for the full retail versions which will include everything needed. Keep this OEM issue in mind when you are shopping online. An Internet store should indicate a product is OEM by marking it as such, as we see here.

Unfortunately, not all do, or may make it difficult to spot. As a result, it is possible to inadvertently pay the full retail price for an OEM component. As ever, buyer beware!

Pre-assembly Checklist

Components

The components required depend on the computer's intended capabilities. At the very least, you will need the following:

- System Case
- Central Processing Unit (CPU)
- Motherboard
- Memory (RAM)
- Power Supply Unit (PSU)
- Hard Drive

- Monitor
- Graphics System
- Sound System
- Keyboard
- Mouse
- Speakers

In this basic setup, the sound system will be built-in to the motherboard and the graphics system built-in to the CPU. For low to mid-level games, these integrated systems will be perfectly adequate.

However, if you intend to use the computer for serious gaming, you will need to buy a dedicated graphics card. With regard to sound, a dedicated card really isn't necessary. In fact, you'd be better off spending the money on a more powerful graphics card or CPU.

Things to Watch Out For

With so many things to take into account, it's almost inevitable than many people forget something or other. The following are typical examples:

1. That the case is large enough to comfortably accommodate the parts you intend to place inside it. If it isn't, assembling the computer may be difficult with an increased likelihood of inadvertently damaging a component. Also, excess heat can be an issue in an under-sized case

2. Still on the subject of heat, check your chosen case has enough fans to keep the system cool. Cheaper cases often come with only one fan, which will not be enough for anything but the most basic system. Two should be the minimum - one drawing air in from the front and one expelling it from the rear

3. If you don't want the expense of a graphics card, make sure the CPU you buy provides integrated graphics. Motherboards these days, don't

4. If you want Wi-Fi in your system, check the motherboard supplies it - not all do. Otherwise, you'll have to add a Wi-Fi card at extra cost later

5. Check the monitor has integral speakers. If it doesn't, you'll need to buy them separately. Similarly with webcams, if you want one

CHAPTER 2

The Central Processing Unit (CPU)

Key CPU Specifications

The CPU is often referred to as the brain of a computer but a more accurate description would be that it is an incredibly fast calculator. Its main function is to take instructions from a peripheral device (keyboard, printer, mouse, etc) or software, and interpret what it requires. It then sends the information to the PC's monitor via the graphics system, or carries out the task requested of it.

This device is one of the most important and expensive components in a gaming computer, and getting the right one is critical. If you don't, your PC will not be what you wanted it to be or will have cost more than it need have done. Maybe even both!

In this chapter, we take an in-depth look at the various factors that will determine your choice of CPU. We'll start with the specifications you need to consider:

Cores

The first CPUs were single-core devices, which meant they could only carry out one instruction, or task, at a time. This was fine, given the undemanding applications around at the time. As software programs became more complex and needed more processing power though, these early CPUs simply weren't up to the job.

The solution was to add another processor, or core, to the CPU. This doubled its capability. Fast forward to the mainstream models of today and even budget CPUs now have four cores, with top-end CPU's having twelve. The more cores a CPU has, the greater the number of independent tasks, or threads, it can carry out simultaneously. In other words, the more powerful it is.

Multi-threading

Multi-threading takes the core concept a stage further by creating virtual CPUs that, to the operating system, are extra physical CPUs. Each of these virtual CPUs can handle another task (or thread) simultaneously, thus improving the real CPU's multi-tasking capability. Intel's version of multi-threading is called Hyper-Threading, while AMD calls theirs SMT (Simultaneous Multi-Threading).

The extra processing power provided by multi-threading is an important consideration for gamers as gaming can be a very resource-intensive activity.

...cont'd

Clock Speed

This metric is measured in gigahertz (GHz), and is the speed at which the CPU operates. As each task carried out by the CPU needs at least one clock cycle, it follows that the higher the clock speed, the more tasks it can carry out in a given period.

Modern CPUs automatically adjust their clock speeds depending on the task at hand and their internal temperature. This is reflected in the specifications which will show a minimum (base) and a maximum (turbo) clock speed.

Turbo Mode

Resource-light applications don't require the CPU to be running at it's maximum speed (and in the process drawing more power and producing more heat). In this situation, the CPU runs at its normal, or base, speed. However, when a heavy-duty application is run, the CPU increases its speed in response to the extra demands being made of it.

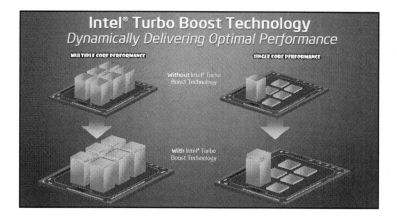

This happens automatically and the clock speed is raised as high as necessary up to a specified limit. The CPU's Turbo Mode specification will show what this limit is. Intel's implementation of the technology is called Turbo Boost, while AMD calls theirs Turbo Core.

Instructions per Clock Cycle (IPC)

CPUs have a set number of instructions that they can process per clock cycle. This is known as their IPC and the specification is manufacturer and/or architecture-specific.

Take two CPUs with the same clock speed and number of cores, from two different manufacturers, and the IPC figures will differ. The same applies if they're from the same company but built on different architectures. This shows that a higher clock speed doesn't necessarily mean better performance. For example, a CPU with a clock speed of 3.5 GHz that can process one million instructions per clock cycle will not perform at the same level as one running at a slower 3.0 GHz but processing two million instructions per cycle.

A CPU's core count, clock speed and IPC are all critical elements in its design and, together, they define its speed and power.

Thermal Design Power (TDP)

A CPU's TDP specification indicates the maximum amount of heat the device is likely to generate when under load. For example, Intel's Core i CPUs have a TDP of 125 watts.

We mention TDP here because it can be the cause of confusion. Some buyers incorrectly assume it indicates the amount of power the CPU draws from the power supply unit. In reality, the figure is used by manufacturers of CPU cooling systems as a nominal value on which to base their systems. The higher its TDP, the more cooling a CPU will need.

Cache

When looking at a CPU's specifications, you'll notice one called Cache. This is an area of high-speed memory, the purpose of which is to act as a temporary holding place for frequently accessed data. This eliminates the need for retrieving the data repeatedly from the slower system memory, thus giving overall system performance a noticeable boost.

CPU cache is split into three sections - Level 1, Level 2 and Level 3. L1 is the fastest and is used for the most frequently accessed data. Typically, it has a storage capacity of 256 KB. In top-end CPUs, it can be as much as 1 MB.

The L2 cache is larger in size (up to 6 MB) but slower in speed, while the L3 is larger still (up to 64 MB) and slower than L2.

Note that the figure given in CPU specifications for cache size is always for Level 3.

CPU Manufacturers

Many people are under the impression that the CPU market is restricted to Intel and AMD. This is not the case at all though, as companies such as Qualcomm, Broadcom, Apple, Samsung, Texas Instruments, NVidia and IBM also make CPUs, albeit for different sectors of the market. For example, phones and tablets. Many other types of consumer device also contain CPUs.

However, it is true to say that Intel and AMD have the market for the CPUs used in desktop computers to themselves. Both companies currently produce three versions of their mainstream CPUs - budget, mid-range and top-end.

Intel

For those of you with deep pockets, Intel's premium offering is the Core X processor. This is an 18 core beast designed for extreme applications such as servers, motion graphics, game development and 3D animation. The computer game that can fully utilise its enormous power will be a long time in the making so, for gamers, it really would be overkill. That's assuming the price didn't kill them first! This thing is mega-expensive.

Intel's mainstream CPUs are the 10th generation Core i9-10900, Core i7-10700 and Core i5-10600. These range in power and capabilities and cover all segments of the desktop computer market. For the gamer, they are a far more realistic proposition.

Core i9

The Core i9 is Intel's flagship CPU for desktop computers and looking at its awesome specifications, it's not difficult to see why:

- Cores - 10
- Threads - 20
- Clock Speed (Base) - 3.7 GHz
- Clock Speed (Turbo) - 5.3 GHz
- TDP - 125 watts
- Socket - LGA 1200
- Cache - L1 - 64 KB, L2 - 256 KB, L3 - 20 MB

The i9 is a very powerful CPU and will be of interest to hardcore gamers and for applications such as video editing and 3D rendering. According to Intel's advertising blurb, it is the fastest gaming CPU on the market.

Core i7

Moving down a step, the Core i7 is Intel's midrange CPU and costs much less than the i9.

- Cores - 8
- Threads - 16
- Clock Speed (Base) - 3.8 GHz
- Clock Speed (Turbo) - 5.1 GHz
- TDP - 125 watts
- Socket - LGA 1200
- Cache - L1 - 64 KB, L2 - 256 KB, L3 - 16 MB

Although less powerful, Intel's i7 CPUs are still serious performers and are more than adequate for the vast majority of applications. This includes most computer games, especially when coupled with a good graphics card.

Core i5

Reaching the bottom of the 10th generation pile, we have the i5. This is Intel's budget CPU and is priced accordingly.

- Cores - 6
- Threads - 12
- Clock Speed (Base) - 4.1 GHz
- Clock Speed (Turbo) - 4.8 GHz
- TDP - 125 watts
- Socket - LGA 1200
- Cache - L1 - 64 KB, L2 - 256 KB, L3 - 12 MB

As you can see, the i5 CPU is the least powerful of the Core i range. Although a very capable processor that can handle most tasks thrown at it, for the serious gamer, it doesn't cut the mustard - he/she will need an i7 or an i9.

The Intel Generation Gap

When looking at Intel CPUs, you will come across Core i processors stretching back years, each of which has a different build architecture. At the time of writing, the most recent (and the one we recommend) is the 10th generation Comet Lake. As already mentioned, these CPUs are the Core i5-10600, the Core i7-10700 and the Core i9-10900.

Previous generations, e.g. Coffee Lake, although still perfectly good CPUs, are yesterdays technology and we'll disregard them for that reason. If you're building a new computer, gaming or otherwise, you want the latest components and, with regards Intel CPUs, that means 10th generation models.

...cont'd

AMD

For many years, AMD's CPUs were considered to be inferior to those from Intel. Today, the situation is rather different. Indeed, with its new Ryzen 3000 series, AMD have finally levelled the playing field. In fact, for certain types of application, their CPUs are now marginally *superior* to Intel's equivalents.

We'll have a more detailed look at the differences between AMD and Intel later but for now let's see what AMD has to offer.

Its equivalent of Intel's Core X CPU is the Ryzen™ Threadripper™ 3990X. As its name suggests, this is a monster of a CPU that has a whopping 64 cores and a matching amount of virtual cores. It isn't intended for the desktop market where, as with the Core X, it would be overkill.

For mainstream users, AMD has the following:

Ryzen 9 3900X
Aimed at the top-end of the desktop market is the Ryzen 9 3900Z, where it competes with Intel's Core i9-10900. As you can see, this is a seriously well specified CPU, particularly in the core count.

* Cores - 12
* Threads - 24
* Clock Speed (Base) - 3.8 GHz
* Clock Speed (Turbo) - 4.6 GHz
* TDP - 105 watts
* Socket - AM4
* Cache - L1 - 768 KB, L2 - 6 MB, L3 - 64 MB

Thanks to its extra cores and threads, the Ryzen 9 has the edge over the Core i9 at multi-tasking. The latter is better for gaming and applications that only require a single core.

Ryzen 7 3800X
Next in AMD's CPU line-up is the Ryzen 7 3800X. A mid-range processor, it is up against Intel's Core i7.

* Cores - 8
* Threads - 16
* Clock Speed (Base) - 3.9 GHz
* Clock Speed (Turbo) - 4.5 GHz
* TDP - 105 watts
* Socket - AM4
* Cache - L1 - 512 KB, L2 - 4 MB, L3 - 32 MB

...cont'd

The performance of the 3800X is on a par with the Core i7.

Ryzen 5 3600X
This CPU competes with Intel's Core i5 at the budget end of the CPU market.

- Cores - 6
- Threads - 13
- Clock Speed (Base) - 3.8 GHz
- Clock Speed (Turbo) - 4.4 GHz
- TDP - 95 watts
- Socket - AM4
- Cache - L1 - 384 KB, L2 - 3 MB, L3 - 32 MB

As with the others, the 3600X performs at a similar level to its Intel competitor and, as such, isn't suitable for a serious gaming computer.

Intel or AMD
Benchmarks show quite clearly that Intel's Core i9-10900 is currently the fastest mainstream processor on the market and the one most suitable for serious gamers. However, AMD's Ryzen 9 3900X is only slightly behind and the difference is not enough to be a deciding factor - that's more likely to be the price as the Ryzen 9 is considerably cheaper. Where the Ryzen range does have a slight advantage is in multi-tasking applications, such as video editing.

The mid-range CPUs from both manufacturers are good enough to play most games on the market.

All the Ryzen CPUs are supplied with a bundled cooler. However, as with most things that are "free", they are not of the greatest quality.

All the CPUs in Intel's Core i range have a version with integrated graphics. The Ryzen 9 CPUs do not.

All the Ryzen CPUs support the forthcoming PCIe 4 standard. Intel CPUs do not.

All recent AMD CPUs can be overclocked. With Intel's though, only models with a K at the end of the name can be. For example, Intel Core i9-10900K.

To summarise, go with Intel CPUs for the very best gaming performance. If cost is a factor, AMD CPUs are nearly as good but cost less.

CHAPTER 3

Motherboards

Motherboard Layout

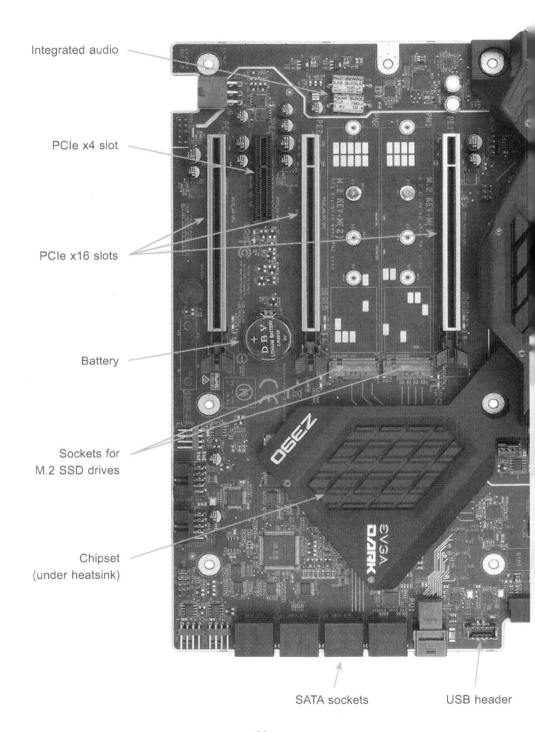

Integrated audio

PCIe x4 slot

PCIe x16 slots

Battery

Sockets for
M.2 SSD drives

Chipset
(under heatsink)

SATA sockets

USB header

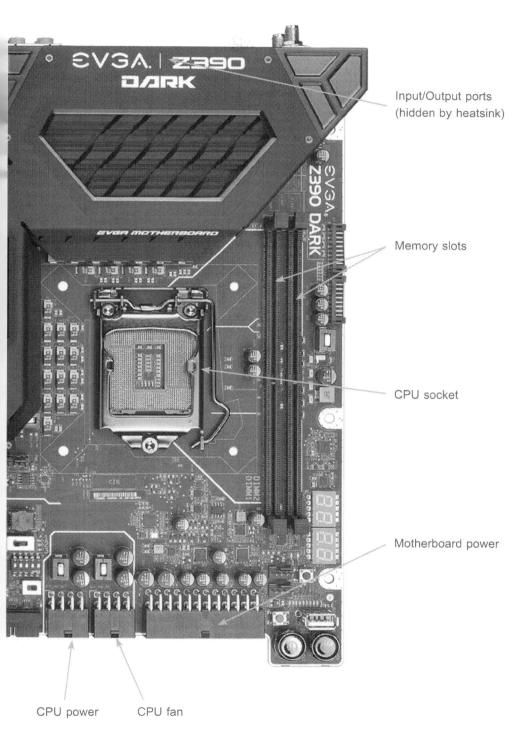

Input/Output ports
(hidden by heatsink)

Memory slots

CPU socket

Motherboard power

CPU power   CPU fan

Motherboard Features

The motherboard plays a central role in any computer system. Every other part is connected, directly or indirectly, to it. Accordingly, the decision of which one to buy is crucial. In this chapter, we tell you everything you need to know in order to get the right board for your machine.

Looking at the motherboard on pages 28/29 will give you an idea of the various functions provided by these boards. Let's take a brief look at what they do:

- CPU socket - the motherboard provides a large socket in which to install the central processing unit

- Memory - motherboards generally provide either two (dual-channel) or four (quad-channel) slots for the memory modules

- Chipset - this manages the flow of data between the CPU, memory, storage and peripheral devices

- Drive sockets - motherboards provide sockets for SATA hard drives and SSD drives. The latest motherboards also provide sockets for M.2 SSDs

- Input/Output Ports - located at the top-left of the motherboard, these provide a means of connecting external devices

- Expansion slots - motherboards can accept a variety of devices which include sound cards, graphic cards and network cards, etc. To this end, they provide expansion slots of various sizes

- BIOS - also known as UEFI in more recent motherboards, this is a chip that controls the computer's boot routine by loading the operating system from the system drive. It also provides a number of low-level settings and functions

- Integrated systems - all motherboards provide a built-in sound system and some older ones provide a built-in graphics system. These eliminate the need for dedicated graphic and sound cards. Other functions that can be integrated include RAID, Wi-Fi and network controllers

- Battery - In older PCs, a battery was needed to maintain power to CMOS RAM (a volatile memory type) that was used to store BIOS settings. With modern PCs, these settings are now stored on non-volatile memory which doesn't need power. However, the battery is still required to keep the PC's clock accurate

CPU Socket

When looking at which motherboard to buy, you should have already decided which CPU you're going to use. The two have to be physically compatible, i.e. the board must provide the correct socket for the CPU.

This is easily established by looking at the relevant specifications. The CPU's specs will show the required socket, while the motherboard's specs will show the socket provided.

Alternatively, you can go to the CPU manufacturer's website. Both Intel and AMD provide system-building guides that make the job even easier. Intel's guide is shown below:

MANUFACTURER RECOMMENDED MOTHERBOARDS TO SUPPORT INTEL® CORE™ i9®

Based on the robust Intel® Core™ i9-9900K architecture, the Intel® Core™ i9-9900KS is a special edition, halo processor featuring even more performa on all 8 cores, right out of the box; 16 threads; 127W; 40 platform PCIe lanes.

Compatible with existing Intel® Z390 chipset-based motherboards, the Intel® Core™ i9-9900KS integrates into a broad selection of motherboards ava performance, Intel® recommends updating the system BIOS to the latest version provided by the manufacturer to ensure the latest power optimizatio

The table below highlights a selection of motherboards that manufacturers have recommended to pair with the Intel® Core™ i9-9900KS Special E

Contact the manufacturer for additional recommendation details.

Manufacturer	Model Name
AsRock	Z390 Taichi
AsRock	Z390 Taichi Ultimate
AsRock	Z390 Phantom Gaming X
AsRock	Z390 Phantom Gaming-ITX/ac
ASUS	ROG MAXIMUS XI EXTRME
ASUS	ROG MAXIMUS XI FORMULA
ASUS	ROG MAXIMUS XI APEX
ASUS	ROG MAXIMUS XI HERO
ASUS	ROG MAXIMUS XI HERO
ASUS	ROG MAXIMUS XI HERO (WI-FI)
ASUS	ROG STRIX Z390-E GAMING
EVGA	EVGA Z390 DARK

Select the CPU and you will be presented with a list of compatibe mother-boards from all the various manufacturers.

Form Factors

Amongst other things, as we shall see, a component's form factor relates to it's physical dimensions. Currently, with regard to motherboards, there are three in common use: ATX, Micro ATX and Mini ITX. These are shown below:

Mini (6.7" x 6.7")

Micro (9.6" x 9.6")

ATX (12" x 9.6")

ATX is the largest and the one best suited to a high-end gaming rig. This is because ATX boards have plenty of space to accommodate the extra and more powerful hardware required by a gaming computer.

For example, they will have four PCIe x16 slots which allows two or more graphics cards to be fitted for much improved performance. Instead of two or four memory slots, they can have as many as eight.

There will be more PCIe x1 and x4 slots which allows other devices, such as sound cards to be added. An ample supply of these slots can also be very handy further down the line should you subsequently decide to expand the computer's capabilities.

Most gamers, however, will be better off with a Micro ATX board as they provide everything needed to build a powerful computer - up to three PCIe x16 slots and four memory slots - but are smaller and cost less. Note that the smaller size makes it easier to use a smaller (and less expensive) mid-tower case.

Mini ITX boards aren't suited to a gaming PC due to their size constraints. They also happen to be the most expensive.

Memory

The memory you choose for your gaming PC has to be compatible with the motherboard in the following ways:

1. The motherboard must support the type of memory being installed

2. The motherboard should support the memory's speed

3. The amount of memory installed should not be more than the board can support

Currently, the type of memory in use is DDR4. All recent motherboards are designed to accept this so it really shouldn't be issue. However, if for some reason, you intend to use an older board, make sure it supports DDR4. Also, don't make the mistake of buying DDR3 memory and trying to install it in a recent motherboard - the slot will be a different type so it won't fit.

DDR4 memory modules are available in speeds from 2400 MHz up to 4000 MHz. Again, any recent motherboard will support this range of speeds. However, it's not the end of the world if you get this wrong. For example, if you install a DDR4 module with a rated speed of 3400 MHz into a board that supports a maximum of 3000 MHz, the module will work but only at 3000 MHz. Effectively, you'll have wasted money.

There's no point installing more memory than the board is designed to use. You may be able to install four 16 GB modules but if the motherboard can only handle a maximum of 32 GB, the other 32 GB will just sit there doing nothing. Having said that, most recent boards support 64 GB, and some 128 GB, so this is only likely to be an issue if you decide to use an older board for some reason.

Chipset

In the early days of computers, motherboards contained a number of chips, each one devoted to a specification function - mouse, keyboard, graphics and so on. This made for a slow and inefficient system.

As motherboard technology improved, all these chips were integrated into just two. These were called the Northbridge and the Southbridge. The former handled all the high speed components - CPU, memory, etc, while the latter took care of slower elements, such as expansion slots, USB ports, integrated audio and graphics, etc.

The next stage of the chipset's evolution saw responsibility for the system's memory and integrated graphics handed over to the CPU. The motherboard's remaining functions were handled by just a single chip - the chipset as we know it today.

Put simply, the chipset is the motherboard's communication centre and traffic controller rolled into one. It determines what components can be used with the board and also sets its expansion options and to what extent the system can be overclocked.

To a large degree, when you are looking at a motherboard's specifications, you are looking at the chipset's specifications.

Chipsets	Supported CPUs	Socket
Comet Lake (10th generation) Z490	10th generation Intel Core	LGA 1200
Coffee Lake (8th gen) H310, B360, H370, Q370, Z370 Coffee Lake (9th gen) Z390, B365, B360	8th & 9th generation Intel Core	LGA 1151
X299	Skylake, Kaby Lake X	LGA 2066
TRX40	3rd gen AMD Ryzen Threadripper	sTRX4
X399	AMD Ryzen Threadripper	sTR4
A300, A320, B350, B450, X370, X470, X570	AMD Ryzen, 7th gen A-Series & Athlon	AM4

Above, we see the most commonly used chipsets and the CPUs they support. Understanding how they work is not particularly important as long as you realise the motherboard must have the right chipset for the CPU you intend to use. Currently, the Z490 is the chipset of choice for Intel-based gaming PCs and the X570 for AMD-based gaming PCs.

Drive Sockets

Current motherboards provide three different types of socket. Note they tend to be called after the interface they use.

USB

External drives connect to USB sockets (or ports), at the rear of the system case. Most cases will have a couple at the front as well.

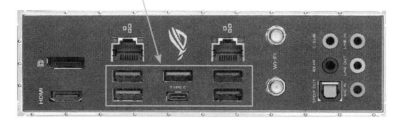

SATA

Drives that use this now common interface are hard disk drives (HDDs) and solid state drives (SSDs). Most motherboards these days provide six SATA sockets, with high-end boards providing between eight and twelve.

M.2

M.2 SSD drives plug directly into a M.2 socket. This is a relatively new type of connection and all recent motherboards will provide at least one. Higher-end boards usually provide two.

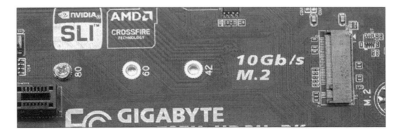

Input/Output Ports

A computer's input/output ports are the assortment of connections located at the top-left of the motherboard. These allow peripheral devices, such as printers and keyboards, to be connected to the computer. A typical example from a modern motherboard is shown below:

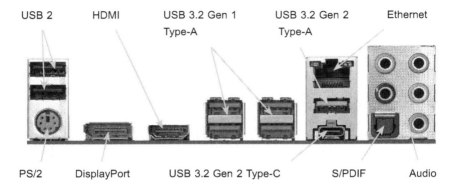

Lets start with the old. The PS/2 port is a legacy port designed to connect mice and keyboards. Although still found on some motherboards for backward compatibility, it has been superseded by USB for a long time now.

USB 2 is now twenty years old and has a maximum transfer speed of 480 Mbps. Although painfully slow compared to USB 3, which is ten times as fast, it is still perfectly adequate for mice and keyboards.

The newer USB 3 comes in several versions:

- USB 3.2 Gen 1 Type-A can transfer data at a maximum of 5 Gbps
- USB 3.2 Gen 2 Type-A can transfer data at a maximum of 10 Gbps
- USB 3.2 Gen 2 Type-C can transfer data at a maximum of 20 Gbps

DisPlay and HDMI ports are used to connect a monitor, or monitors, to the computer. Each has its pros and cons - see page 86.

The Ethernet port connects the computer to network devices such as routers and modems.

The five audio ports are for stereo speakers, 4-channel speakers, 5.1-channel speakers, 7.1-channel speakers and headphone & microphones.

S/PDIF (Sony/Philips Digital Interface) is an audio cable format that allows the transfer of digital audio signals without the need to convert to an analog signal first. It is little used these days.

Expansion Slots

Just as its input/output ports enable devices to be connected externally, a motherboard's expansion slots enable devices to be connected internally.

Over the years, there have been quite a few types of these; PCI, PCI Express, AGP, ISA, AMR and CNR being just some. Because many of them have been in use at the same time, it has made building and upgrading computers unnecessarily complicated. Fortunately, things are much simpler today as there is now just one type to deal with - PCI Express (PCIe).

Currently, the most common PCIe standard is PCIe 3.0, although PCIe 4.0 is now available on the latest Ryzen-compatible motherboards. Note that each new version of PCIe is twice as fast as its predecessor. Also, they are all backward compatible so devices built for early versions will still work on the newer ones, albeit at a slower speed.

PCIe slots come in four sizes - x1, x4, x8 and x16, with the size dictating the data transfer speed of the connected device. The ones most commonly used are the x1, x4 and x16 slots.

| x1 | x4 | x8 | x16 |

The larger the slot, the faster it's data transfer speed. For this reason, all graphics cards use the x16 slot. Motherboards designed for use in gaming machines will provide at least two of these, which enables multi-GPU setups.

The x1 slot is commonly used by small form factor devices, such as sound cards, networking cards and port expansion cards (cards that add extra connections - USB and Thunderbolt, for example).

Cards that typically use the x4 slot include PCIe to M.2 adapter cards, and RAID cards that enable two or more drives to be set up in configurations that improve performance and data security.

Devices that use the PCIe x8 slot are few and far between.

Note that x1, x4 and x8 expansion cards can all be connected to a x16 slot, and x1 and x4 cards can be connected to a x8 slot. This means you have more options with regard the devices that can be installed on the motherboard. For example, if you have two devices that use the x4 slot but there is only one of them, you can connect the second device to a spare x8 or x16 slot.

UEFI BIOS

The term BIOS is short for Basic Input/Output System and refers to a program installed in a chip on the motherboard that provides low-level control for the computer's hardware. Because it is built-in to the system, its settings don't change when the computer is powered off.

When a computer is switched on, the BIOS starts up, initialises the system's hardware and checks that everything is working as it should. This is known as the power-on self-test (POST). It then identifies which drives have an operating system installed and loads the one that is set as the default. After that, the operating system takes over.

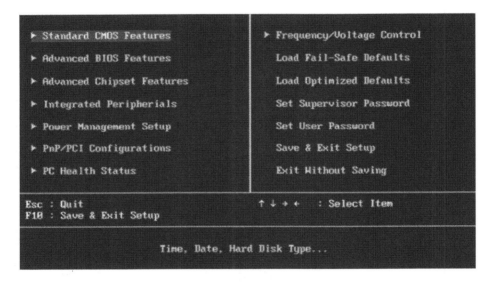

As can be seen from the example above, traditionally, BIOS programs have provided little in the way of features other than some basic system configuration settings and changing of the boot order.

More recent motherboards come with a much improved version of the BIOS, which is known as UEFI (Unified Extensible Firmware Interface). This is a far more comprehensive program that offers a wealth of features, many of which will be of particular interest to the gamer. Just some of the advantages EUFI offers include:

* Support for hard drive partitions larger than 2 Tb

* Faster boot and shutdown speeds

* More efficient power and system management

...cont'd

- A secure startup routine that ensures malware cannot interfere with the startup procedure

- A much richer user interface that provides far more information and setup options as we see in the example below:

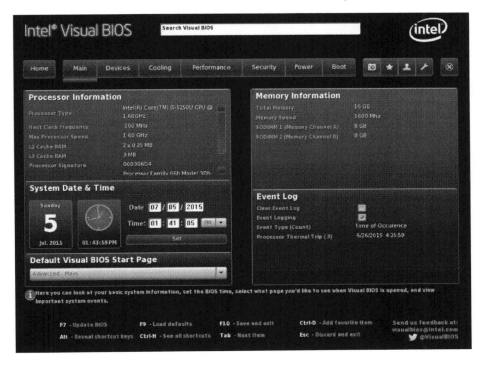

The UEFI provides detailed information on all the hardware in the PC - CPU, memory, motherboard, drives, etc. This can be useful in a number of ways. It also enables you to monitor the system to make sure everything is running smoothly. For example, you can check the speeds and temperatures of the CPU and memory and, if necessary, make adjustments.

For power users, there will be an overclocking utility that forces the CPU, memory and graphics card to run at higher speeds than they were designed to. The aim here is to squeeze more performance out of them. We'll take a closer look at this in Chapter 13.

A RAID utility is another UEFI feature that can be useful. For example, two drives in a RAID 0 configuration will run at double their rated speed. This may be of interest to gamers looking for performance gains wherever possible.

You will also need the UEFI to install Windows as we explain on pages 111-114.

Integrated Systems

Traditionally, motherboards have provided built-in, or integrated, systems that save the user having to buy dedicated devices. This is both convenient and cost-effective. Typically, these have been sound, graphics and networking systems, with some boards also providing an integrated RAID controller.

More recent motherboards, however, have seen changes in what's provided. While they all still offer a sound system, this is no longer so with graphics. These days, integrated graphics have shifted from the motherboard to the central processing unit. This means the self-builder has to either buy a dedicated graphics card (which will be the case in most gaming rigs) or make sure the CPU they buy comes with integrated graphics.

All motherboards provide Ethernet functionality that enables the computer to be physically hooked up to the Internet. This is not the case with Bluetooth and Wi-Fi - many motherboards don't provide either so this will need checking in the board's specifications.

Are these integrated systems any good, though? Well, in the case of sound, the answer is a definite yes. Capable of supporting 7.1 sound, an integrated sound system will be good enough for most users. Serious gamers and dedicated audiophiles may beg to differ.

Things are not so clearcut with video. While the majority of games will run on an integrated system, they may not do so all that well, particularly at high settings. Resource-intensive games with high frame rates will definitely require a graphics card. The only way to be sure about this is to check the specifications of both your games and the graphics system you are thinking of using.

Integrated Ethernet will be perfectly adequate as will Bluetooth and Wi-FI (if provided). A dedicated network card will only be needed if the computer is to be part of a local network. Note that there are "gamer network cards" on the market that claim to improve gaming performance by reducing network latency (lag). In our experience, these have little or no effect and are largely a waste of money.

Turning to RAID, as integrated RAID controllers are hardware-based, they are much more reliable than software-based RAID controllers, such as the one provided by Windows. They can, however, be somewhat limited in functionality in which case a dedicated RAID controller card may be needed.

CHAPTER 4

Memory

What is Memory?

A computer's memory takes the form of an oblong circuit board on which are mounted a number of memory chips. The chips themselves consist of capacitors and transistors, a pair of which creates a memory cell that can hold a single bit of data. Each of these chips has literally millions of cells.

Here, we see a basic memory module:

And below we see the same thing but this time encased in a heatsink, the main purpose of which is to keep the memory module cool. These devices, particularly the high-performance modules used in gaming machines, can produce a lot of heat.

A secondary purpose is ascetics - to make the gaming rig look "cool". This is something that's popular with many gamers.

The role of memory is to provide the computer with a short-term data storage system. It works by storing data that's currently, or frequently, being used so it can be quickly accessed again when necessary. This makes it possible to run several applications concurrently, and rapidly switch between them. For example, you can have a web page and your email program open at the same time you're playing a game, i.e. multi-tasking.

Your applications and data are stored on the PC's drive. When you open one of those applications, its data is transferred to the memory and then on to the CPU. The more memory you have, the greater the amount of data that can be quickly accessed by the CPU. And, of course, the faster the memory, the faster the transfer rate.

So, as you can see, the memory plays an important part in a computer's multi-tasking capabilities and overall speed.

Types of Memory

There are quite a few different types of memory, each designed for specific segments of the memory market. For example, error-checking memory is used in servers where reliability is critical. Others are SRAM and DRAM. The buyer will also come across terms like dual-channel and quad-channel.

The memory technology currently in fashion is Double Data Rate Synchronous Dynamic RAM, or DDR for short. This is a version of DRAM and virtually all desktop computers use it as it's fast and reliable. SRAM is even faster and for this reason is used as cache memory in CPUs.

DDR memory is available in four versions: DDR1, DDR2, DDR3 and DDR4, with DDR1 being the oldest and DDR4 the newest. Each successive version has made improvements in terms of speed, power requirement (which in turn leads to less heat produced) and operating efficiency.

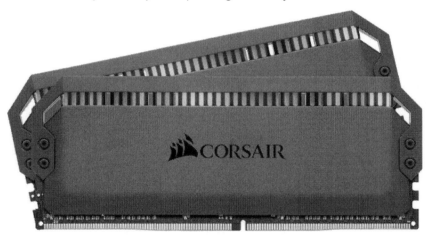

We won't waste any time on DDR1 and DDR2 as they really are yesterday's technology. DDR4 may be the latest and greatest but it is also the most expensive. This means there is still a place for the cheaper DDR3 as the performance differential between them is negligible.

However, should you consider buying DDR3 as a means of cutting costs, be aware the two are not interchangeable. Motherboards designed for DDR3 will not accept DDR4 modules and vice versa. So by going with DDR3, while you may save money, you are committing yourself to old technology.

For the gamer who is intent on building a high-performance machine, the only option is DDR4 memory. However, if all you play is budget and mid-range games, DDR3 will be quite adequate, as long as you're prepared to put up with the limitations it will bring.

Memory Specifications

By the time you start investigating the memory market, you should have already decided what level of gaming machine you want, i.e. budget, mid-range or an "all guns blazing" monster, and chosen your CPU and motherboard accordingly. This is important, as to get the best out of your memory it must be compatible with, and able to work on the same level, as these two components.

The following specifications are the ones you need to look at:

Capacity
The amount of memory that you require in your machine is determined by the games, and simultaneous applications such as the operating system, that you intend to run. The table below shows the memory requirements for some of the currently most popular games:

Game	Memory Needed
Phantom Brigade	16 GB
F1 2019	16 GB
Far Cry 5	8 GB
Shadow of the Tomb Raider	8 GB
Crysis 3	8 GB
Final Fantasy XV	8 GB
Vampyr	8 GB
Kingdom Come: Deliverance	8 GB
Rise of the Tomb Raider	6 GB
Assassins Creed Origins	6 GB
Just Cause	4 GB
Minecraft	4 GB
Enemy Front	3 GB
World of Warcraft Classic	2 GB
Arkham City	2 GB
Orcs Must Die	2 GB
Darkest Dungeon	2 GB
Into the Breach	1 GB

...cont'd

The memory requirement specification for all games can be found at the manufacturers websites. Usually, they will be quoted as "minimum" and "maximum". Our recommendation is that you go with the maximum amount suggested. We say this for two reasons:

1. The game will run with the lower amount but may well struggle at the highest settings

2. You will inevitably have other applications running concurrently, which will also be using the memory

Memory modules are available in capacities of 4 GB, 8 GB, 16 GB, 32 GB, 68 GB and 128 GB. The latter three are far more than any game could possibly need, while 4 GB is only enough for low-end titles. As you can see from the table on page 44, the vast majority will run perfectly well with 8 GB or less. It's only top-end games that will benefit from 16 GB.

As a final word, given that memory is one of the cheaper components in a computer, there's little point in skimping on it. Get what you know you will need with a bit extra as overhead.

Speed

As with other system components, memory speed is measured in MHz. The figure is usually listed immediately after the DDR version, i.e. DDR4 3200 and enables you to match a memory module to the CPU and motherboard in this respect.

Memory modules are currently available at speeds of 2400 MHz, 2666 MHz, 3000 MHz, 3200 MHz, 3600 MHz and 4000 MHz. Our recommendation is to go with 3000 MHz, or 3600 MHz if playing resource-intensive games.

How important is memory speed though with regard to gaming? The answer is that it depends on the game and the graphics engine. For recent releases, it is a factor but not for older games. Even so, it doesn't make that much of a difference. The amount of memory is usually more significant.

Where memory speed does have more of an impact is when an integrated graphics system is being used rather than a dedicated graphics card. But, as you're building a gaming machine here, you shouldn't even be thinking about integrated systems!

Latency

Latency is the time lag between a data request being made and the data being delivered, and it is measured in clock cycles.

...cont'd

Due to the way it is presented (as four numbers, e.g. 16-17-167-35), it can be a confusing specification to understand. However, the only number you need to take note of is the first one. This represents the number of clock cycles the memory takes to send a piece of data to the CPU.

Memory Series	DOMINATOR PLATINUM RGB
Memory Type	DDR4
Memory Size	64GB Kit (4 x 16GB)
Tested Latency	18-22-22-42
Tested Voltage	1.35V
Tested Speed	3600MHz

In the example above, taken from the Corsair website, the memory module has a latency of 18. Many manufacturers just list the first number.

The lower the latency, the better. When looking at this specification, you may notice that the older DDR3 modules are actually faster in this respect. Typically, they'll have a latency of between 6 and 10, whereas with DDR4 it's between 15 and 19.

This is a side-effect of the higher bandwidth found in DDR4 memory. However, the much faster clock speed of DDR4 more than compensates for the higher latency so, overall, it is still faster than DDR3.

Multi-channel Memory

This is basically a method of increasing the memory's bandwidth, the act of which enables the system to run more quickly and efficiently. The process is operated by a memory controller built-in to the CPU which handles the flow of data throughout the computer.

Memory controllers have a number of channels with which to communicate with the memory. The more channels there are, the faster data moves through the system. Currently, memory controllers are built with one channel, two channels (dual-channel), four channels (quad-channel), six channels, and eight channels. Of these, dual-channel and quad-channel are the ones that will be used in a gaming computer. One channel is yesterday's technology and six-channel and eight-channel are for use in data-intensive servers.

Multi-channel memory architecture also needs to be supported by the mother-board. Furthermore, the memory modules have to be identical and they must be installed in matching slots. In most motherboards these days, the slots are colour-coded to this end.

The memory manufacturers all sell kits that contain the required number of modules, and that match in terms of speed, capacity and latency. Our advice is that you go with one of these kits as it ensures you don't make a mistake. Note that should you install modules that don't match, the memory will still work but only at the speed of the lowest rated module.

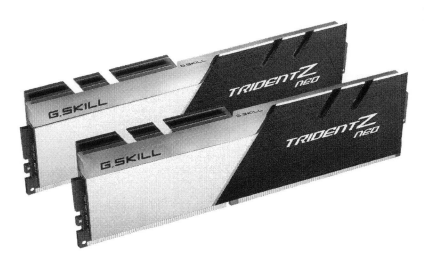

You would be forgiven for assuming that a quad-channel setup will be twice as fast as a dual-channel one. After all, it has twice the number of channels with which to transmit data - how can it not be? The reality, however, may surprise you. Very few people will see a noticeable performance gain from a quad-channel configuration for the simple reason mainstream programs and the vast majority of computer games simply don't need the huge bandwidth it provides. Dual-channel is perfectly adequate for them.

This may not be the case with games still in the pipeline though. Successive editions of most applications, including games, nearly always need more in the way of system resources. Future-proofing your computer is the only reason we can see for a quad-channel setup. You'll get much more of a performance gain by going for a dual-channel setup and spending the money saved on a faster CPU or drive.

XMP and AMP

When you come to set up your newly built gaming computer (see Chapter 11), you may notice that the memory is running at a lower speed than the headline figure stated on the box. For example, if it's rated at 3000 MHz, it will be running at about 2600 MHz.

The reason for this is that memory modules are supplied at a "safe setting" - a performance profile that's a bit under their maximum. This is to ensure they work correctly out of the box and don't cause the system-builder any problems.

To get it running at the rated speed, you need to change a setting in the BIOS. With Intel systems, the setting is called XMP and with AMD systems, it's called AMP. Essentially, it's a controlled method of overclocking the memory.

We explain how to do this on page 116.

CHAPTER 5

Graphics Systems

Types of Graphics System

A computer's graphics system takes the stream of 0's and 1's from the CPU and arranges them into an intelligible picture on the monitor. Two types are used - integrated graphics and dedicated graphics cards.

Lets take a closer look:

Integrated Graphics (iGPU)

An integrated graphics system is one where the graphics processing unit is built-in to either the motherboard or the CPU. They're small, don't need much in the way of power and are cheap. These characteristics make them ideal for low-power devices, such as tablets, phones and laptops, where graphics processing requirements are low.

However, being small doesn't necessarily mean they don't pack a serious punch - some of them do. Enough, in fact, to handle the graphics requirements of desktop PCs. High-end integrated graphics systems will be found in PCs from the big manufacturers like Dell, Hewlett Packard, Apple, etc. The current trend is to build them into the CPU rather than the motherboard.

Some of the CPUs in Intel's Core i range come with its UHD Graphics 630 iGPU. AMD's Ryzen range is available with its Vega 11 Graphics. Of the two, the Vega 11 Graphics is generally considered to be the better performer.

All low-end, and most mid-range, games will run perfectly well with either of these iGPUs. There are some, though, that will need the settings to be turned down. Neither of them are good enough for serious gaming, however.

Graphics Card (GPU)

Dedicated graphics cards provide a much higher level of video quality than integrated systems do. With their own processor and memory, they are designed with speed as one of the main criteria and provide features that are geared specifically to getting the best out of resource-intensive games.

For the gamer, this component is even more important than the CPU. Unfortunately, the process of buying one can be intimidating as there's so much to consider. For example, the type of monitor, the specifications, the games themselves, not to mention the price - these can be very expensive pieces of equipment!

To complicate the issue even further, graphics cards are the most hyped part of a computer system. Many people get taken in by it and end up buying an expensive model that provides a level of performance they will never need. Then there's the wide range of graphics card manufacturers from which to choose.

...cont'd

Companies such as ASUS, MSI, Gigabyte, Sapphire, EVGA, XFX and Powercolor all manufacture products that are very closely matched in terms of features and specifications.

You will also see references to two other companies - AMD and Nvidia - and it's these you need to pay more attention to. They are the only companies that actually make graphics processing units (GPUs). All the companies that market graphics cards, build them around the GPUs that AMD and Nvidia produce.

Take the following cards for example:

- Gigabyte Geforce RTX 2080 Super Windforce OC 8192 MB GDDR6
- MSI Geforce RTX 2080 TI Gaming X Trio 1126 MB GDDR6
- ASUS Geforce RTX 2080 TI ROG Strix OC 11264 MB GDDR6

They may be three different cards from three different manufacturers but they are much the same because they all use Nvidia's Geforce RTX 2080 GPU chip. Where they differ is in the build quality and the specifications of ancillary components, such as the onboard memory.

AMD and Nvidia both market several versions of each chip they produce to cater for the low-end, mid-range and high-end sectors of the market.

Graphics Card Specifications

When in the market for a graphics card, the following specifications are the ones you need to consider:

Onboard Memory

The amount of memory the card provides is the most important specification of all as it makes high resolutions possible, and also allows graphics quality to be set at high levels. The minimum needed for full HD (1920 x 1080) gaming these days is 4 GB. If you're gaming at very high resolutions, such as 4K, the minimum is 8 GB. For future-proofing purposes, it makes sense to consider 10 GB, or even higher.

However, bear in mind that a graphics card's memory is only effective if the application being run can actually use it. Everything else being equal, a game that runs perfectly well with 4 GB of memory, won't run any better with a card that has 6 or 8 GB.

Memory Speed

High-speed graphics memory increases the speed and performance of a graphics card in the same way high-speed system memory does for the computer. Low-end cards come in at around 7000 MHz, mid-range cards at 10000 MHz and the latest high-end cards at up to 15000 MHz.

Memory Type

The type of memory used in graphics cards is an enhanced version of the Double Data Rate (DDR) memory used as the main system memory and is called Graphics Double Data Rate (GDDR) memory. This has been optimised for use with video and the current version is GDDR6. This runs at twice the speed of it's predecessor, GDDR5.

GDDR6 also has a lower power consumption and is available in higher capacities. Note that many graphics cards on the market use the slower GDDR5, so keep a lookout for this.

Cores

Just like CPUs, the processors used in graphics cards are equipped with a number of cores. However, whereas a CPU is a general-purpose device designed to handle various types of application, a GPU has just one purpose - the processing of video. To this end, GPUs have literally hundreds, or even thousands, of cores all focused on video. For example, Nvidia's RTX 2080 Ti has no less than 4,352 of them.

As with most things to do with computing devices, higher numbers almost always equate to better performance. This definitely applies to GPU core-count.

...cont'd

Nvidia calls their GPU cores "Cuda Cores" while AMD calls theirs "Stream Processors". Due to differences in the GPU architectures used, the two are not directly comparable. An Nvidia card with, say, 3000 Cuda cores will not necessarily offer the same level of performance as an AMD card that has 3000 Stream Processors.

Clock Speed

As with the CPU, a GPU's clock speed is the measure of how many processing cycles it can execute per second. While not the most important specification regarding performance, it should, nevertheless, be taken into account. A good graphics card will have a clock speed of at least 1000 MHz. Top-end cards will be nearer 2000 MHz.

Graphics cards can be overclocked to increase their clock speed and boost performance. Typically, any gain will be in the region of 10 percent or so. However, this might require more cooling to be added to the system and may end up being more bother than it's worth. See pages 144-145 for more on this.

Ports

A graphics card's ports enable it to be connected to the monitor. Modern cards provide three different ports:

* Digital Video Interface (DVI)
* High Definition Multimedia Interface (HDMI)
* DisplayPort

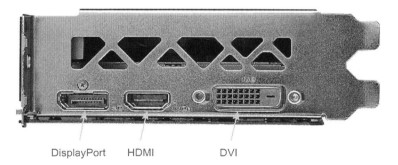

DisplayPort   HDMI   DVI

DVI has been around for years but is still found on many cards for backward-compatibility purposes. Although still capable of providing a good connection, it has its limitations and so is not recommended.

The more capable HDMI and DisplayPort have also been around for years (2002 and 2006 respectively) and are currently the connections of choice. Both have been the subject of numerous revisions, each of which have improved their performance and capabilities. Currently, the latest version of DisplayPort is 2.0 but virtually all graphics cards are still using version 1.4. Similarly with HDMI, the latest version of which, 2.1, has yet to be taken up by the manufacturers who are still using version 2.0.

So which of the two is best for connecting a gaming PC? The answer is that there really isn't much in it. However, because it is designed specifically for use in computers whereas HDMI is a more general-purpose connection also used in consumer electronic devices such as TVs, DisplayPort is the recommended option.

Power Consumption

Graphics cards use a lot of power, particularly at the high-end. In fact, they use as much, if not more, than the rest of the system combined. So to ensure your power supply unit is up to the job, you must check this specification.

Fully loaded, top-end cards need in the region of 350 watts. So when the power requirements of the rest of the system are factored in, a power supply unit providing between 600 and 650 watts will be required. If you intend to overclock your system, you could well need even more, maybe as much as 800 watts.

Size

Graphics cards are serious pieces of circuitry and not just in terms of specifications. They are physically big and take up a lot of room in the case. The cooling systems these cards require (up to three fans) make them even bigger.

While there's no question of them being *too* big to fit in a case, the size of high-end models can block access to adjacent PCIe slots on some motherboards. Take this possibility into account when planning your system.

Graphics Cards Features

Specifications don't tell the whole story regarding a card's capabilities - you also need to take a look at the features built into it.

Multi-GPU Setups

For years now, really serious gamers have been taking advantage of a graphics card technology that makes it possible to run up to four cards simultaneously. This provides an enhanced output for the best possible gaming experience.

AMD's version of the technology is called CrossFire while Nvidia call theirs Scalable Link Interface (SLI). Note that the latter has now been superseded by NVLink - a similar technology that has yet to be taken up by the game manufacturers. Whether it will or not remains to be seen.

Should you consider trying this yourself, our advice is to not bother for the following reasons:

*   Support from the game manufacturers for multi-GPU setups has been waning for several years

*   It's expensive - two or more cards, more power used, more heat produced necessitating extra cooling, and more space needed in the case

*   Many games don't benefit from it

*   It can be tricky to setup and maintain

Settle for a single card - the best one you can afford. Adding more is usually more trouble and expense than it's worth.

Virtual Reality (VR)

VR is a technology that provides a truly immersive, first-person perspective of game action. Gamers access and influence the game environment via a variety of VR devices and accessories. These include VR headsets, sensor-equipped gloves, hand controllers, and more.

The two main VR platforms for gaming computers are HTC Hive and Oculus Rift. To use either, you will need a mid-range graphics card at the minimum. For the best performance, a card such as the RTX 2060 Super will be required.

Ray Tracing

Ray tracing has been used for years in the movie industry to simulate photo-realistic lighting and shadow effects. It hasn't been available to gaming machines, though, due to the enormous computing power it requires.

However, Nvidia's new Turing range of GPUs come equipped with ray tracing cores that do provide the necessary power, and thus herald the introduction of a technology considered to be the Holy Grail of the gaming industry. Quite simply, ray tracing games will be much more immersive and offer a visually stunning experience.

While there are quite a few other graphics cards on the market that have limited support for ray tracing, only the latest RTX cards from Nvidia have the power to implement the technology properly. Be warned, though - these are expensive and will probably only be of interest to the hardcore gamer.

Games that can take advantage of ray tracing are currently limited but the list is growing rapidly. Some that do include Battlefield V, Shadow of the Tomb Raider, Quake II and Metro Exodus.

Other Considerations

4K Resolution Support

Currently, most games have a maximum resolution of 1080p, also known as Full HD. However, some now run at 4K. This is a much higher resolution that provides far more detail, and thus offers a more realistic gaming experience.

If you intend to play these high-res games, you must make sure your graphics card is up to the job. While most modern GPUs can handle 4K, they may not do so particularly well, particularly with the game settings turned up. To get the best from these games, a top-end graphics card will be needed.

Heat

Graphics cards are powerful devices and generate a lot of heat which they are designed to cope with under normal conditions. However, when conditions aren't normal, as they won't be in an under-sized case or when overclocked, the card may well overheat. If it does, while it will probably keep on running and you will be blissfully unaware of the issue, the life of the card may be shortened considerably.

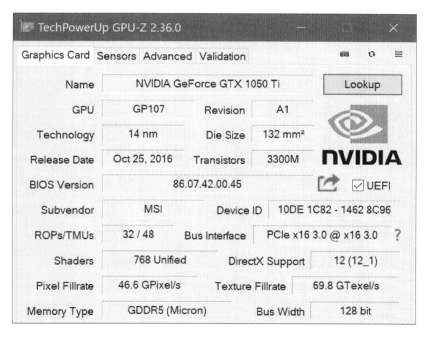

So, in either of the above scenarios, we recommend that you monitor the card with a suitable utility, a good example of which is GPU-Z. Designed specifically for use with graphics cards, it is a positive mine of graphics-related information. Other utilities you can use include Geeks3D GPU Shark, Open Hardware Monitor, GPU Temp and CPUID Hardware.

AMD or Nvidia

As we mentioned on page 51, while there are many companies busily engaged in the production of graphics cards, they all build their cards around GPUs from Nvidia and AMD. Intel is proposing to enter the graphics card market in September 2020 with its XE Graphics GPU, but, until it does, this remains an unknown quantity. In any event, it's unlikely to be a serious competitor right from the off.

So, given that AMD and Nvidia both make cards that cover all sectors of the market, which one do you go for? The answer in our opinion, is largely determined by the following factors:

- The games you play
- Price
- Future-proofing

Let's start with the games. If they are resource-intensive, such as Far Cry 5 or Warhammer 2, you need to be looking at the top-end of the market. This means you will be buying an Nvidia card from its RTX range for the simple reason AMD offers nothing to match it. However, with budget and mid-range games, there is no clear favourite. There is little to distinguish between cards built around either company's GPUs for these markets.

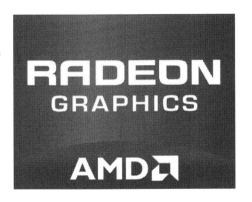

This takes us on to price, which will likely be the determining factor for most people in the budget and mid-range markets. However, as with the cards themselves, there is little to choose in terms of price as both companies are competing fiercely in these lucrative sectors. In the end, it may come down to grabbing the best discount you can find.

Ensuring your card can handle the latest technologies, and those still in the pipeline, will be the deciding factor in some cases. A typical example here is Ray Tracing technology which, as we've seen, is set to take the gaming world by storm. Does it make any sense for the serious gamer to settle for a card that isn't capable of utilising this exciting new development?

CHAPTER 6

Power Supply

Power Supply Units

The power supply unit takes the alternating current from the wall socket and converts it into the range of voltages required by the various components in the computer. It is without doubt the least interesting of all the parts and, for that reason, it's easy to overlook its importance. Doing so is potentially a big mistake, however, and can give rise to problems down the line.

A common misconception with these devices is they are the part most likely to fail and that when they do, they send a surge of current through the system that can damage other components. This may have been true years ago (and still is with cheap models of dubious origin) but modern, good quality, PSUs are no more likely to fail than any other part. Even if they do, they are built with fail-safe circuitry designed to shut them down and prevent damage to external components.

Cheap PSUs, on the other hand, are not. For this reason, it is essential that you get a good quality model from one of the main manufacturers. It won't make your gaming machine any faster but it will ensure the power that runs it is stable and up to the job. It is definitely not a component to cut costs on!

To make sure you get the right one for your system, we recommend you spend as much time evaluating the power supply unit as you do with all the other components.

Specifications

There are a number of specifications you need to look at when buying one of these devices. These include:

Power Rating

PSUs are rated in watts and range from about 400 W at the bottom end of the market to 1000 W or so at the top-end. If you're building a powerful gaming machine, you're going to need one with a power rating of at least 500 W.

To work out the power requirements of your PSU, you have two ways to go. The first is to use an online calculator, such as the one from ASUS below:

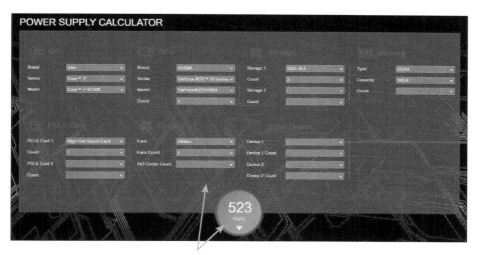

Simply specify your components and click the Calculate button to see the required power rating.

Alternatively, check the power specification of each component to see how much it requires, then add them up. Whichever way you do it, be sure to buy a PSU of a higher rating. For example, if you calculate you will need a 500 W PSU, get one rated at 550 to 600 W. There are three reasons for doing this:

- Running a PSU continuously at full load is a guaranteed way of shortening its expected lifespan

- PSUs are more efficient when they are run at medium load

- Having power in hand will allow you to add extra devices later or upgrade an existing one

Note that a PSU will only output the power being asked of it. It may be rated at, say, 850 W but if the system is only asking for 350 W, that's what it will deliver.

Efficiency

Another measure of a PSU's performance is its efficiency rating. This is determined by comparing the power going into it with the power coming out. The difference is the amount of power lost as heat.

Thus, the less efficient a PSU is, the more expensive it is to run. To illustrate this, consider a PC that needs 300 W of power. A PSU with an 85 percent efficiency rating will draw about 350 W from the AC supply. A PSU that's only 70 percent efficient, on the other hand, will draw about 430 W.

More important, however, is the heat generated by inefficient PSUs. This raises the operating temperature not only of the PSU itself, but also the PC. The long-term effect will be a reduction in the PSU's, and possibly the PC's, working life. With this in mind then, you need to get a PSU with an efficiency rating of at least 80 PLUS. 80 PLUS is a certification program that manufacturers use to prove their PSUs meet a minimum efficiency level, i.e. at least 80 percent.

The program has various levels as shown in the table below:

% of Rated Load	10%	20%	50%	100%
80 PLUS	-	80%	80%	80%
80 PLUS Bronze	-	82%	85%	82%
80 PLUS Silver	-	85%	88%	85%
80 PLUS Gold	-	87%	90%	87%
80 PLUS Platinum	-	90%	92%	89%
80 PLUS Titanium	90%	92%	94%	90%

This makes it easy to find a PSU that's suitable for your gaming machine. Our recommendation is nothing less than 80 PLUS Gold.

Overload Protection

Good quality PSUs incorporate fail-safe circuitry that prevents damage to other components in the system should they fail. These circuits monitor the voltage, current and heat levels of the PSU and if any of them exceed a designated limit, the PSU will automatically shutdown rather than blowing as cheaper models are likely to.

This is a very important feature as all power supply units, no matter how good, will eventually fail.

...cont'd

Good PSUs also offer protection against voltage surges in the external AC supply. Cheap PSUs don't and so should be avoided. The output voltages of these low-cost units also tend to fluctuate, particularly under heavy loads. This can be the cause of general system instability that can result in freezes, crashes and sudden reboots.

So when making your choice, check the specifications and make sure they include protection circuitry.

Form Factors

A power supply unit's form factor determines its size, shape and outputs. It also ensures that its fixing holes line up with those of the case.

When checking out these devices, there are two main standards the buyer will come across. One is the ATX12v form factor and the other is the EPS12v form factor. The latter is designed for use with servers and requires PSUs to be built to a very high standard due to the demands made by server environments.

The ATX12v form factor is designed for desktop computers and is the one the gamer will be interested in. PSUs built to this standard will fit in both full-size and medium-size cases.

Connectors

Having established that your chosen PSU has the required power and efficiency ratings, and the correct form factor, the next thing to look at is the connections it provides. The following are the ones you can expect to find in a modern power supply unit:

 The **24-pin ATX** connector is the largest of the PSU's connectors and is used to power the motherboard. There will be just one of these.

 The **4-pin ATX12V** connector supplies 12 volts and is used to power budget CPUs. Just one is provided.

 The **8-pin EPS12V** connector also supplies 12 volts to the CPU. This connector is used by mid-range and top-end CPUs. There will usually be two cables each providing one connector.

...cont'd

The **6-pin PCIe** connector supplies 12 volts to mid-range graphics cards.

The **8-pin PCI-E** (6 + 2) connector supplies 12 volts and is intended for top-end graphics cards. There will usually be four cables, each providing two connectors.

The **4-pin Molex** connector is used to power the case fans. There will usually be two cables, each providing two or three connectors

The **SATA** connector is used to power drives. There are usually four cables, each providing three or four connectors

Many of these connectors (and the cables they're on) won't be used. However, they must all, nevertheless, be accommodated inside the case. This means tucking them in wherever possible. The cables are thick and heavy and not only look messy, they can interfere with airflow within the case.

This problem can be avoided by using a modular PSU as shown above. With these, the cables have connectors on both ends and you just plug in the ones

you need to use. Or, you can opt for a semi-modular model in which the main cables (24-pin ATX, 8-pin EPS12V and 8-pin PCIe) are built-in (native). All the others plug in (modular).

External Power Supply

Something else the gamer might care to consider is the AC supply to the computer. Because it's always there and always works, few people ever give it a thought. This is a mistake though as AC power supples are prone to a number of issues that can cause problems with computers. These include:

- Line noise
- Power surges
- Frequency variation
- Under and over voltage levels

Every computer user will, at one time or another, experience all of the above and never be aware of the fact as, typically, they last for just fractions of a second. However, they do cause PCs to freeze and crash, which is something the gamer definitely does not want to happen in the middle of an intense piece of action.

The solution is to invest in a surge suppressor. These devices iron out any sudden variation in the AC signal and ensure the input to the power supply unit is rock solid.

A good model will also be capable of removing line noise and distortion in the AC signal, thus delivering a "clean" supply.

Other Considerations

Multiple GPU Support

On page 55, we looked at the issue of running up to four graphics cards simultaneously to gain enhanced performance. Should you be thinking of trying this, don't forget that the PSU must provide the necessary support.

With some PSUs, the specifications state clearly that multiple GPUs are supported. Others, however, don't and with these you need to be careful. Check the PSU's output is sufficient to power all the graphics cards, plus the rest of the system.

Continuous Wattage v Peak Wattage

Some PSU manufacturers advertise their products with two power output figures - Continuous or Max, and Peak, which can be confusing for the uninitiated. The former is the figure you need to take note of as it specifies the power a PSU can deliver continuously without fluctuations. The Peak figure refers to the maximum power it can deliver for a short period before dropping down to a safe level.

Rails

When looking at PSU specifications, you'll notice these devices are available in single-rail and multi-rail versions. With single-rail PSUs, all the power is available from a single source - the rail. This means that if there are any problems with the incoming AC supply, the output from the rail may be adversely affected. With multi-rail PSUs, however, this problem is eliminated as the PSU's output is split across the rails.

For the vast majority of users, a single-rail PSU is the one to go for. It's only people who live in areas where the AC supply is unreliable that need to use a multi-rail model.

High Power Output Doesn't Mean High Quality

There are a lot of companies engaged in the manufacture of PSUs and they all use the power rating as the main selling point. However, with some of these companies, while their PSUs may deliver the quoted power for a while, they may not do so for very long.

As already stated, our advice is to stick with reputable companies such as Corsair, EVGA, CoolerMaster, Antec, Silverstone, Thermaltake and Seasonic. Give the others a miss (particularly those of far eastern origin).

CHAPTER 7

Cases

Types of Case

For the vast majority of computer users, the case is the least considered part of a PC, being just a box that houses the components. Usually, it is tucked away in a corner or under the desk and rarely given a thought.

Gamers, however, have another use for it as it gives them an opportunity to make their machine look the part. To this end, instead of being plain and featureless, many gaming cases are actually very stylish and colourful. We take a look at the issue of case aesthetics on page 72.

Essentially though, cases are there to provide a protected environment for the computer's components. They come in two basic types - Desktop and Tower. The former are used in small form factor computers and are not suitable for gaming PCs due to their size constraints.

For the gamer, therefore, tower cases are the way to go. These are available in three main sizes - mini, mid and full. Mini towers are similar to desktop cases in terms of size and so are a non-starter. Mid- and full-size tower cases, however, are both compatible with the ATX standard and so fit the bill.

The only problem with mid-tower cases is that they provide a limited amount of space. That said, for budget and mid-range gaming computers that don't have huge graphics cards, heat sinks and water cooling systems, they are perfectly adequate.

The components in top-end machines, however, are simply too bulky and so a full-size tower case will be the best option. These cases are massive and provide all the space needed for even the most highly specified gaming PC. As we will see, an adequate amount of space is essential, not only for fitting the parts but for airflow that will keep the system cool, and efficient cable management.

Case Features

There are a number of things to consider with regard to buying a case for a gaming computer. These include:

Capacity

As we have just seen, the general rule is that top-end gaming computers need a full-size case and low and mid-range ones a mid-size case. However, while this is the recommended way to go, it is possible to fit a top-end rig in a mid-size case should you wish to do so. You may not want to sacrifice the amount of desktop space a full-size case will occupy, for example.

In this situation, you need to check the dimensions of three things:

- Graphics card
- CPU heatsink
- Liquid cooling radiator

Top-end graphics cards can be very long devices and, depending on the design, can be difficult to fit in a mid-size case. While we're not saying this is likely to be a problem, it is worth checking out just to be on the safe side.

The same applies to CPU heatsinks, only this time in terms of height. Some CPU heatsinks are taller than others and not every mid-size case has the depth to accommodate them. Make sure this isn't going to be an issue by checking the specifications - the case's specs sheet should specify the maximum CPU heatsink height it can accommodate.

Liquid cooling systems use liquid to transfer heat from CPUs and GPUs to a radiator. These systems come in a range of sizes and, in a mid-size case, are the most likely cause of installation problems.

Cooling

The typical desktop computer doesn't require high-spec components and so heat is rarely, if ever, an issue. The same can't be said of gaming machines, particularly those with powerful graphics cards. These produce serious amounts of heat which, if not safely dispersed, will be the cause of components failing well before they should do. The computer may also be prone to instability issues and throttling of key components such as the CPU.

To address this issue, the self-builder has three options. The first, and most obvious, is to buy a good quality gaming case. These are designed to optimise air flow, and include two or more good quality fans, both of which reduce heat levels in the case.

Secondly, if the case isn't up to the job, there is always the option of adding extra, or larger, fans to increase the amount of cooling. To this end, most modern gaming towers have several mounting points for extra fans. When doing this, it is important to ensure a balance, i.e. that there is an exhaust fan for every intake fan. If not, you risk creating a negative pressure system which can make things worse rather than better.

Typically, intake fans are placed at the front or bottom of the case while exhaust fans are placed at the rear. Note that the direction in which the fans are installed determines whether they act as an intake or exhaust fan. Make sure you read the instructions and get this right.

The final option is to install a liquid cooling system - an example is shown above. Typically, these comprise a pump to move coolant through the system, a radiator that releases heat into the air, fans that blow air over the radiator, and hoses that connect it all up.

Liquid coolers come in three types: closed-loop, open-loop and all-in-one. Of these, open-loop cooling systems are far and away the best but are expensive and installation can be complex.

Noise

An unwelcome side-effect of fans is the noise they produce. In a highly specified gaming computer they can be loud enough to be distracting. One way of dealing with this is so-called silent fans. These are available for system cases, CPUs and graphics cards. While not truly silent, they are quieter.

Something to be aware of here is that the fans on graphics cards, which are the worst offenders for creating noise, can be difficult to replace.

Another noise reduction method is soundproofing. Many gaming cases are available already soundproofed but, if you have decided on a case that isn't, you can buy a soundproofing kit and do the job yourself. These take the form of self-adhesive mats that you simply cut to size and stick in place. You can also buy kits that have been pre-cut to fit many popular cases.

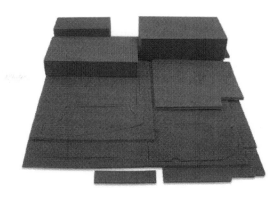

When considering this option, bear in mind that soundproofing mats can be up to half an inch in thickness and may reduce the internal dimensions of the case considerably.

Construction

Cheap gaming cases tend to be flimsy as they use thin, low-grade, steel which also has poor heat transfer properties. Good quality cases are constructed of higher-grade steel and are much sturdier. At the top end of the market, cases are made from aluminium which has more efficient heat dispersal properties.

Another construction feature found on many top-end gaming cases is built-in compatibility for liquid cooling systems. These tend to be found on full-size tower cases and simplify the installation of these cooling systems considerably.

Good quality cases also attend to the issue of dust by including filters to keep the inside of the case as clean as possible. Dust is an insulator and, over time, can accumulate and contribute to the build up of heat.

Cable Management

While not mission-critical, keeping the computer's cables tucked neatly away doesn't just make for a more professional looking job, it actively assists in maximising the flow of air in the case.

To this end, you should look for a case that offers plenty of holes through which to thread cables, and hooks to attach them to. Also useful is space behind the motherboard which can be used to route cables out of the way.

Those of you who like a really clean look can invest in a PSU shroud. This is basically a cover that conceals the cables coming out of the PSU.

Aesthetics

Gamers spend a lot more on their rigs than the average computer user would ever dream of doing for the simple reason that modern games demand a powerful and thus expensive setup. For many, having done so, it make sense to pay a few dollars more to make sure everyone who sees it is in no doubt they are looking at something special.

Never slow to spot a market, all the case manufacturers have a range of cases designed to appeal to image-conscious gamers. These come in many different shapes and sizes as we see in the examples below:

Apart from their often outlandish appearance, these cases are, in the main, of an extremely high build quality and will be able to accommodate all types of setup.

A feature common to most of them is a transparent side panel that reveals the guts of the machine. This creates an incentive for the gamer to customize the inside of the case as well with RGB LED lighting. Motherboards, memory sticks, PSUs, graphics cards, case fans and CPU coolers are all available with this type of lighting.

And if your case still isn't bright enough, you can add more pyrotechnics with RGB lighting kits. Many of these kits include control panels and enable customized lighting effects to be created.

It won't be cheap but if you want your gaming machine to be lit up like the Vegas Strip, everything you need to do it is available.

CHAPTER 8

Drives

Types of Drive

There are various types of drive, each of which have strengths that make them suitable for some purposes and weaknesses that make them less so for others. We'll start with drives intended for internal use.

Hard Disk Drives (HDDs)

The oldest type of drive in current use, HDDs are electro-mechanical devices that employ spinning platters coated with a magnetic material to store data, and moving actuator arms that do the reading and writing.

The main problem with these drives is that they are slow and, for this reason, are not suitable for use as the main system drive in a gaming computer. That said, they do have two big advantages over newer and faster types of drive. The first is that they are cheap and the second is they are available with massive storage capacities of up to 12 TB. In comparison, the latest SSD drives have a maximum capacity of 2 TB.

This makes HDDs ideal for storing large game files which can be loaded onto the faster system drive as and when needed.

Hybrid Drives (H-HDDs)

A hybrid drive is essentially a mechanical hard drive that has been given a speed boost by adding a flash memory cache of the type used in SSDs. Typically, this will be around 64 GB in size. You may notice that the drive specifications give this figure in MiB rather than GB. The difference between the two is negligible enough to be ignored, however.

In operation, frequently used data is stored in the memory cache and because this type of memory is so fast, when the data is accessed again, the drive is able to respond much more quickly than an ordinary mechanical drive would.

Effectively, hybrid drives are nearly as fast as an SSD while, at the same time, providing much greater, and much cheaper, storage capacity. In terms of performance, they slot in between top-end HDDs and SSDs.

A step-up from hybrid drives are the more recent solid state hybrid drives

(SSHDs). With these, the cache memory has been replaced by a small SSD. They work the same way but with better performance due to the faster SSD.

Solid State Drives (SSDs)

Unlike HDDs, SSDs have no moving parts. Instead of a spinnng platter, they store data on NAND flash memory chips. Because they don't have to wait for a platter to move into place, these drives are much more efficient.

SSDs offer a number of advantages over the older HDDs. These include:

* Speed - SATA SSDs are three to four times as fast as HDDs. PCIe SSDs are even faster

* Response - SSDs start instantly. This gives faster boot times, faster application loading and better overall system responsiveness

* Noise - as SSDs have no moving parts, they are silent in operation

* Durability - SSDs are more durable, and thus reliable

* Footprint - SSDs are smaller and lighter than HDDs

* Power - SSDs require much less power than HDDs

These drives are available in two different types and are named after the interface they use. Hence, we have SATA SSDs and PCIe SSDs. The ones most commonly used are the SATA models that connect via the SATA interface with a cable.

However, due to the bandwidth limitations of the SATA interface, SATA SSDs are not able to achieve the speeds that SSD technology is capable of. This brings us to PCIe SSDs. These drives plug into a PCIe slot on the motherboard and so can utilise the higher bandwidth provided by the PCIe interface. As a result, they are much faster than SATA SSDs. An example from ZOTAC is shown below:

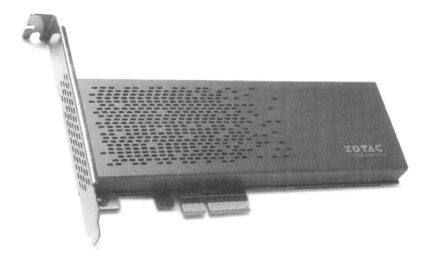

The drawback with PCIe SSDs is that they are bulky and, by taking up a PCIe slot, they limit the PC's expansion options. To overcome these issues, a newer type of SSD has been developed. Known as an M.2 SSD, it connects to the motherboard via a designated M.2 socket.

These drives are very small, typically around 1 x 3 inches, flat and occupy very little space. The M.2 socket is compatible with both the SATA and the PCIe interfaces and, as a result, there are two types of M.2 SSD - SATA and PCIe. Both will only work with the interface they were designed for.

Looking at the Samsung 970 EVO M.2 SSD below, you will notice the letters "NVMe" stamped on the casing. These stand for "Non-Volatile Memory Extension", which is a communication transfer protocol developed especially for SSDs, and indicates the SSD supports it.

...cont'd

This is a complicated issue so we won't get bogged down in detailed explanations but suffice to say NVMe-enabled M.2 SSDs that use the PCIe interface are currently the fastest drives on the market. M.2 SSDs that use the SATA interface are much slower (and much less common).

Moving on to external drives, as with internal models, these come in HDD and SSD versions and have the same advantages and disadvantages. Both types connect via the USB interface and, assuming one of the latest SSD models that use USB 3.1, data transfer rates will be similar to those of internal SATA SSDs.

For the gamer, this fact makes external USB 3.1 drives an ideal solution for gaming on the go. Simply pack the drive in your bag before you leave, connect it at the other end and fire up the game. Because they are so fast, you can play directly from the drive.

External SSDs are available with huge capacities of up to 10 TB, so can also be used for storage purposes.

Most drive manufacturers provide external SSDs aimed firmly at the gamer. While expensive, these not only look the part, they have the fastest speeds, plus features designed to facilitate optimum game play.

Drive Specifications

A fast drive is crucial for a gaming machine. You can have the fastest CPU and memory in the world but, if used in conjunction with a slow drive, overall system performance will be seriously compromised.

The following specifications are the ones to consider in order to get the right one for your system:

Form Factors

SATA SSDs use the 2.5 inch form factor and have to be installed in a drive bay in the case. The much smaller and faster M.2 form factor SSDs connect directly to the motherboard, thus leaving two less cables (interface and power) to have to contend with.

With regard to HDDs and H-HDDS, these come in two form factors - 2.5 and 3.5 inches. The former is designed for use in laptops so if you are considering buying one of these drives, it will have to be a 3.5 inch model.

Interfaces

There have been a number of drive interfaces over the years, each of which have offered more in terms of reliability, speed and features than their predecessors. The ones in common use today are:

SATA - SATA is a development of the old PATA (Parallel Advanced Technology Attachment) interface and has now become the mainstream internal drive interface for hard disk drives (HDDs) and the newer solid state drives (SSDs).

There are three incarnations of SATA. The first, SATA I, had a data transfer rate of 1.5 Gb/s, the second, SATA II, transferred data at 3 Gb/s, and the third, SATA III, has a transfer rate of 6 Gb/s.

The SATA interface can be denoted in three ways: SATA I, II or III as above; SATA I, SATA 2 or SATA 3; and SATA 150, SATA 300 or SATA 600.

PCIe - Small form factor PCIe M.2 SSDs are now increasingly being used in desktop computers. These connect to the PCIe interface via an M.2 socket on the motherboard and, as this interface is designed for use with graphics cards, it offers an incredibly high transfer rate. This allows these drives to fully exploit the incredible speeds made possible by SSD technology.

USB - USB is a plug-and-play interface used to connect external devices to a PC. With regard to storage, it is only used with flash drives and external SSD drives. As with SATA, there are several versions of USB, of which there are currently three in use.

The oldest is USB 2, which has a maximum data transfer speed of 57 Mb/s.

Next is the much faster USB 3 with a maximum transfer speed of 640 Mb/s. Then we have the latest version, USB 3.1, which transfers data at a maximum rate of 1.25 Gb/s.

Thunderbolt - Developed jointly by Intel and Apple, Thunderbolt is an interface designed for use with external devices, including drives. Although superficially similar to USB, it is actually far more capable. The latest version, Thunderbolt 3, has a maximum transfer rate of 10 Gb/s, can charge smart-phones and laptops, and can be used to connect external GPUs.

Typically, the Thunderbolt interface is only found on top-end motherboards. However, it can be added to any computer via an expansion card.

Drive Speed

Firstly, let us clear up what for many people is a confusing issue. This is the distinction between drive speed and interface speed.

Drive speed is the rate at which data is moved from a drive to its interface (be it SATA, PCIe or USB) and is measured in bytes per second, i.e. Megabytes (MB/s). Interface speed (also known as data transfer speed) is the rate at which data is transferred from the interface to the system (and vice versa) and is measured in bits per second, i.e. Megabits (Mb/s).

The maximum speed of current SATA SSDs is around 550 MB/s. SATA M.2 SSDs are the same. PCIe SSDs and PCIe M.2 SSDs are five to six times as fast, i.e. around 3000 MB/s.

With regard to HDDs, drive speed is known as the Data Rate. This comes in two versions - Maximum Data Rate and Sustained Data Rate. The former is the maximum speed under optimal operating conditions and can be disregarded as it will never be achieved in real life. The sustained data rate, however, is an average figure taken under more realistic conditions and is much more representative of a drive's real speed.

A sustained rate of about 150 MB/s is the best you can expect from an HDD. Note that if the data rate version isn't specified, the figure given will be the maximum data rate.

Be aware that, in general, you should take drive speed specifications with a pinch of salt. For the manufacturers, they are a marketing tool and are taken under optimum operating conditions that are never seen in the real world. In practice, any drive you buy will be considerably slower than the manufacturer would have you believe. Real-world drive speed also depends on the data being handled. For example, a drive will transfer four 250 MB files much more quickly than one thousand 1 MB files. The amount of data is the same but there is a lot more system overhead involved with small files.

Disk Speed

This specification is specific to HDDs. As already mentioned, these drives are mechanical devices that use rotating platters. The faster these platters rotate, the quicker the drive can locate and transfer data. The slowest HDDs have a rotational speed (disk speed in the specifications) of 5400 rpm, mid-range models will have a rpm of 7200 and high-end models 10,000-15000 rpm.

Average Seek Time

Another HDD specification to look at is Average Seek Time. This is a measure of the speed with which the drive can position its read/write heads over a data track. The specification is measured in milliseconds and the lower the figure, the better the drive's performance.

Storage Capacity

Standard SATA SSDs are available with capacities up to 8 TB but, at this level, are extremely expensive. Lower capacity models are much more affordable. With regard to M.2 SSDs, these currently have a maximum capacity of 2 TB which is still a huge amount of storage space and should be ample for most users. They are much more expensive than SATA drives of equivalent capacity though - currently by around 50 percent or so.

HDDs are available with capacities up to 14 TB and provide the most cost-effective storage option as they also cost far less than SSDs.

Summary

To sum up, assuming cost is not a factor, the gamer will be best served by a PCIe M.2 SSD, between 256 and 512 GB in size, as the system drive. A second, larger, PCIe M.2 drive (or standard SATA SSD) can be added for storage. Alternatively, a single PCIe M.2 SSD of 1 TB or 2 TB can serve both purposes.

If cost is a factor, go for a standard SATA SSD system drive and a larger SSHD or HDD for storage. While a speed of 500 MB/s doesn't sound as exciting as 3000 MB/s, it's still more than adequate for playing even the most demanding games.

As a final note, even if you don't currently need the insane speed of a PCIe M.2 SSD, investing in one will future-proof your system with regard to drives.

CHAPTER 9

Monitors

Panel Types

A very important factor with gaming monitors is the type of panel used. These come in the following types, each of which have their pros and cons:

Twisted Nematic Film (TN)

TN panels are the most common type. They offer fast response times, typically 1ms, and high refresh rates that remove the trailing and motion blur that can be experienced with fast-moving objects. This makes them a good choice for high-speed games. A bonus is that they are the least expensive type.

The main drawbacks are their restricted viewing angles and the fact that of all the panels, they are the worst at colour reproduction. It should also be noted that very few TN panels support HDR (see page 88).

In-Plane Switching (IPS)

The main advantage of IPS panels is their excellent colour accuracy that produces a saturated and vibrant picture. In this respect, they are a much better choice than TN panels. They also have the best viewing angles of all the panels, and their response time is superior to the majority of VA panels. Indeed, top-end models are just as fast as TN.

Unfortunately, IPS panels suffer from what's known as "IPS glow". This manifests itself as an apparent glowing around the corners of the screen that can be off-putting. The effect is most obvious when viewed at an angle.

Vertical Alignment (VA)

VA panels have the best contrast ratio. This enables them to show deeper blacks which makes it easier to discern details in shadows. Colour reproduction is better than with TN panels and is close to what IPS can achieve, as are viewing angles.

The downside is that they have the worst response time. This can cause ghosting, particularly in dark or black sections of an image. As a result, VA panels are not suited for fast-paced games.

Summary

TN offers decent image reproduction and the fastest response rate at the cheapest price. VA is the least responsive type but offers better contrast and colour performance than TN. IPS panels have the best colour reproduction, excellent viewing angles, good responsiveness and reasonable contrast. They are, however, the most expensive.

So, for most gamers, a TN panel will probably be the choice. However, if your wallet can stand the strain, top-end IPS panels that are just as fast are now available and, given they are superior in all other respects, are the best option.

Screen Size

It goes without saying that the size of the monitor is important with regard to viewing comfort, and that it must suitable for the types of games you play. However, the hardware in your system will be a big factor as well.

An image consists of millions of tiny dots called pixels and the larger the image, the more of them there are. As all these pixels are generated by the computer, it follows that the larger the monitor (and the picture on it), the more powerful the computer needs to be. This applies particularly to the graphics system. If either (or both) isn't up to the job, the result will be a picture that is slow, jerky and that has a tendency to freeze. The monitor's resolution enters the mix here as well - see page 84.

So, when you're at the planning stage, you need to establish that the system is powerful enough to drive the monitor at the desired size and resolution or, in the case of a less powerful system, that the monitor is small enough to compensate for the lack of power.

Common sizes for gaming monitors are 24, 27 and 32 inches, although they can be as big as 49 inches. Many people make the mistake of assuming that bigger has to be better here. However, as pointed out above, the larger the monitor, the more powerful (and expensive) the hardware needed to run it. Nor, for most people, does it add much, if anything, to the gaming experience.

Monitors are also available in ultrawide flat-screen and curved-screen versions, both of which offer an extended field of view. If you're considering one of these, our advice is to go for a curved-screen model. They do a better job of mimicking a three-dimensional space than flat screens do thanks to the curvature that helps improve peripheral vision.

They are also better for your eyes as the curve keeps all images equidistant. This helps the eyes adjust to images at varying distances on the screen, and results in less strain on them.

The main drawback is the cost. Not only are the monitors themselves very expensive, they require a seriously powerful, and thus expensive, PC. Be aware that small curved-screen monitors have less curve and so are not as effective as larger ones.

Specifications

Having decided what type of panel technology is suitable for your requirements, and a suitable monitor size, you now need to take a look at general monitor specifications. The following are the ones you need to consider:

Aspect Ratio

A monitor's aspect, or screen, ratio is the proportion of width to height and is measured in inches. The most commonly used monitors these days are flat wide-screen models that have an aspect ratio of 16:9. Not only does this ratio suit most purposes, it can also adequately display both 4:3 and 21:9 images, albeit with black bars around the edges.

Ultrawide flat-screen and curved-screen monitors, as discussed on the previous page, start at aspect ratios of 21:9 and go as high as 32:9. Most gaming monitors use 21:9.

Resolution

This metric is an important specification and refers to the width and height of the monitor screen in terms of pixels, rather than inches as with aspect ratios.

All monitors are capable of displaying several resolutions. However, they can only display one at high quality. This is known as the native resolution and it indicates the maximum number of pixels a monitor can use in displaying an image. The other resolutions are achieved by a process called interpolation (scaling of the image), which reduces image quality.

Due to this limitation, resolution must be taken into account when deciding what size monitor to buy - it must be one that you are comfortable with and that is suitable for the games you play.

Common resolutions for standard size flat screen monitors are:

* 1280 x 720 - known as High Definition (HD)
* 1920 x 1080 - known as Full High Definition (FHD)
* 2560 x 1440 - known as Quad High Definition (QHD)
* 3840 x 2160 - known as Ultra High Definition (UHD) or 4K

Wide- and curved-screen monitors use a different range of resolutions.

For gamers, it is important to strike a balance between screen size and resolution. For example, low resolution on a large monitor results in a picture that lacks clarity and sharpness, while a high resolution on a small monitor will create a picture in which the elements are small and difficult to discern.

Professional gamers use a 24 inch monitor in conjunction with a FHD resolution of 1920 x 1080 as, overall, this works best. However, if you're prepared to spend the money needed for a more powerful computer, then a 27 inch monitor running a QHD resolution of 2560 x 1440 will be just as good while providing a sharper picture. In our opinion, this hits the sweet spot. It will also future-proof your system as new games are increasingly being optimised for QHD. Be warned though - this will require a top-end graphics card to work well.

Finally, with regard to gaming at 4K resolutions, we really can't recommend this. It will need a seriously powerful and expensive machine, and the improvement over a QHD setup will not be enough to justify the cost.

Refresh Rate

Refresh rate refers to the number of times per second that a panel can refresh an image. The higher the rate, the smoother the on-screen action, particularly in fast-paced action games. A high refresh rate also enables the player to see more detail which can be advantageous in competitive games.

Refresh rates are measured in Hertz (Hz). So a monitor with a refresh rate of 120 Hz will refresh the screen 120 times per second. All monitors are capable of a range of refresh rates with the maximum rate, typically, being 60 Hz. This is fine for standard PC applications and basic computer games. More complex games, however, respond far better with a refresh rate of 144 Hz. In our opinion, this is the minimum you should look for.

For the really serious gamer, monitors with refresh rates of 240 Hz and 360 Hz are available. However, the difference between 144 Hz and 240 Hz is not nearly as pronounced as it is between 60 Hz and 144 Hz. Between 240 Hz and 360 Hz, it is even less.

As with everything to do with graphics, the higher the specification, the higher the cost. So if you envisage a need for high refresh rates, be prepared to shell out for a powerful graphics card as well.

Response Rate

A monitor's response rate is the time it takes for its pixels to go from an active state to an inactive state and back again. It is measured in milliseconds (ms). Basically, it is a measure of how fast the monitor can respond to changes in the data coming from the graphics system.

If the response rate is too slow, the transition from one picture (or frame) to another can result in blurring. With this in mind, choose a monitor with a response rate of as close to 1 ms as you can. Don't go for anything with a rate of over 5 ms. For most games, the latter figure will give acceptable results.

Colour Gamut

A colour gamut, or colour space as it's also known, is the range of colours a monitor can display. Because it can't display every possible colour that humans are capable of seeing, it instead settles for a predefined set of colours. Monitor manufacturers use a variety of these colour gamuts, the most common being sRGB, Adobe RGB, and NTSC. Of these, the most prevalent is sRGB and is the colour format use by Windows, and all the gaming platforms such as the Xbox and Playstation.

However, there's a new kid on the colour gamut block with the catchy name DCI-P3 (Digital Cinema Initiatives – Protocol 3). Developed specifically for use with ultra-HD and HDR, it is estimated to cover about half the colours humans can see as opposed to the one-third that sRGB can. This translates to much richer, saturated colours, and a more pleasing viewing experience.

DCI-P3 has been widely taken up the movie, TV, photography and design industries. The game developers though, who usually lag behind, are still persisting with sRGB as it suits them to do so. However, it's just a matter of time before they will have to adopt this new colour gamut and, in anticipation of this, monitor manufacturers are now making models that are compatible with it.

So, to future-proof your gaming machine in this respect, our advice is to make sure your monitor can display the DCI-P3 colour gamut.

Interfaces

Monitors use two types of connection to the computer - HDMI (High Definition Multimedia Interface) and DisplayPort. They both enable the transmission of high-quality audio and video. Whereas HDMI has been developed as a general type of connection for consumer electronic devices, DisplayPort was developed specifically for use with monitors.

The question for gamers is which of the two to go for and, in truth, it is a difficult question to answer. Specifications-wise, DisplayPort is undoubtedly the more capable. For example, it has a much higher bandwidth than HDMI, and supports multi-streaming (running multiple displays from one port).

However, its superiority really only comes into play when using high-end gaming monitors with refresh rates of 144 Hz and above, and that support G-Sync (see page 87). This can be confusing because while graphics cards from Nvidia and AMD that support these high refresh rates are compatible with both DisplayPort and HDMI, monitors that can display at these levels almost exclusively use DisplayPort. Thus, for gamers who play at resolutions below 144 Hz, it makes no difference which is used - each is as good as the other.

Other Considerations

Adaptive Sync

An issue that plagues many gamers is that of screen tearing. This manifests itself as a horizontal line on the screen with slightly mismatched images above and below it, as demonstrated in the image below:

There are three ways of dealing with this. The first is known as V-Sync and is built into many games. It works by synchronising the game's frame rate with the monitor's refresh rate and does help to reduce screen tearing. V-Sync has limitations though.

Another solution is what's known as Adaptive Sync, of which there are two versions - Nvidia's G-Sync and AMD's FreeSync. Essentially, they both do the same thing as V-Sync - dynamically adjust the monitor's refresh rate in relation to the game's frame rate. However, they do it better.

Given they both do the job, which do you plump for, though? The answer depends on several factors. If you are using an AMD graphics card, it's simple - it has to be a FreeSync monitor. If it's an Nvidia card, you will need either a G-Sync monitor that has controlling hardware built into it, or a FreeSync monitor that can be adapted by installing a GeForce driver from Nvidia.

G-Sync monitors provide a reliable gaming experience. FreeSync, on the other hand, is an open-source software solution, the efficiency of which depends on the monitor's manufacturer. In other words, it's inconsistent as it relies on how well the manufacturer implements the FreeSync technology. With cheaper gaming monitors, it may not be very good at all. Then there's the cost - G-Sync

...cont'd

monitors are more expensive due to the hardware controller. With FreeSync there's no cost to the monitor manufacturer that has to be passed on to the consumer.

On a final note, be aware that G-Sync will only work with the DisplayPort interface. FreeSync will work with both DisplayPort and HDMI.

High Dynamic Range (HDR)

Essentially, HDR is a technology that improves contrast ratio, i.e. the distinction between bright and dark areas of an image. Furthermore, HDR monitors with a wider colour gamut, such as PCI-P3, are capable of producing more vivid and colourful images.

For it to work, the game must support HDR. Those that do include Destiny 2, Battlefield 5, Far Cry 5 and Metro Exodus, to name a few. However, most games released prior to 2017 don't have HDR support.

CHAPTER 10

Assembling the Computer

CPU

Installing the CPU on the motherboard is the first step and has to be done before the board is fitted inside the case. This is because the second step, fitting the CPU's cooler, requires access to the back of the motherboard. The procedure is as follows:

Unhook the CPU socket's locking lever to release the load plate.

Lift the load plate to reveal the socket.

...cont'd

Position the CPU using the alignment marks and place it in the socket.

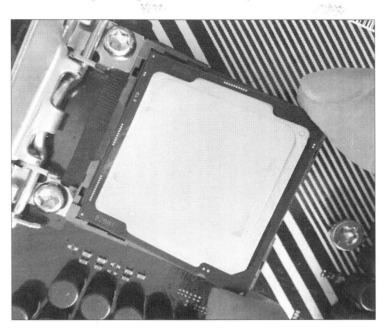

Lock the CPU in place with the load plate by re-engaging the locking lever

CPU Cooler

The CPU's cooling system consists of a heatsink and fan. The most common method of attaching it to the motherboard is by screwing it to a mounting plate located on the rear of the board. Attaching this plate is the first step. Some are a push-fit as shown below, while others screw in place.

Before you can attach the heatsink, you need to apply a pea-sized blob of thermal paste to the top of the CPU. This improves the transfer of heat to the heatsink and will be supplied with the CPU.

...cont'd

The base of the heatsink will have two or three screw holes in each corner. Establish the ones required.

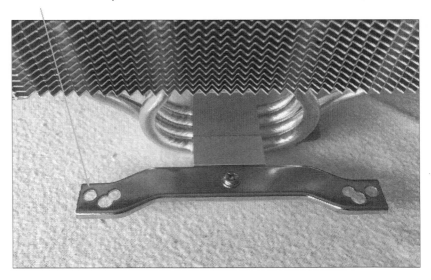

Carefully position the heatsink onto the CPU, lining up the screw holes at the base with those of the mounting plate. Then secure the heaksink in position.

The heat sink's weight will spread the paste over the entire surface of the CPU, thus ensuring optimum heat transfer.

Memory

The first step is to open the clips on either side of the slots you intend to use.

To ensure the memory module fits correctly, align the cut-out on it's edge connector with the engaging lug on the slot.

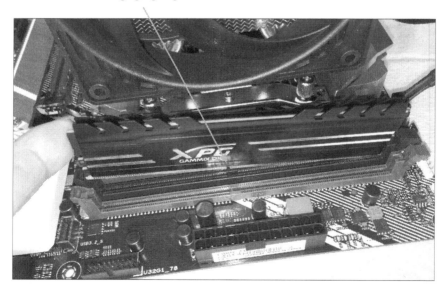

If you are fitting a dual or quad-channel memory set, refer to the motherboard's manual for which slots to use.

...cont'd

Press down on either end until the module clicks into place. The retaining clips will close automatically.

Repeat the procedure if you are installing more than one module. In our system, we are using two 8 GB modules in a dual-channel configuration.

M.2 SSD Drive

M.2 drives connect to a small socket that lies flat to the motherboard. There will be either one or two of them on all recent boards and they are usually located near to the memory slots.

Take the standoff supplied with your M.2 SSD and screw it into the hole on the motherboard. Then remove the securing screw at the far end of the socket.

Push the M.2 SSD into the socket with a finger. It will go in at an angle of around 30 degrees.

Now push the drive down so that the notch at the end lines up with the securing screw hole. Replace the screw to fix the drive in place.

With some motherboards, the M.2 socket will be concealed by a heatsink as we see below. Simply unscrew it, fit the drive and then replace the heatsink. However, if your drive is supplied with an integral heatsink, use that instead.

Motherboard

Supplied with your motherboard will be an assortment of screws and other bits and pieces. In a plastic bag, you will find six to nine stand-offs. There will also be an input/output shield, the purpose of which is to provide protection for the motherboard's ports - these are located at the top-left of the board.

The input/output shield will either snap or slide into place. Be careful as the edges can be sharp.

Input/output shield in place.

...cont'd

Now locate the fixing holes on the case's side panel that correspond to those of the motherboard and screw the stand-offs into them. You can do this with your fingers - they don't need to be particularly tight.

With that done, you're ready to secure the motherboard in the case. Take some care when doing this as it's very easy to damage the underside of the board with the stand-offs. Line them up with the board's screw holes and then screw the board down with the supplied screws.

Graphics Card

Most graphics cards these days are double height, so to fit them you will need to remove two PCIe slot covers at the back of the case.

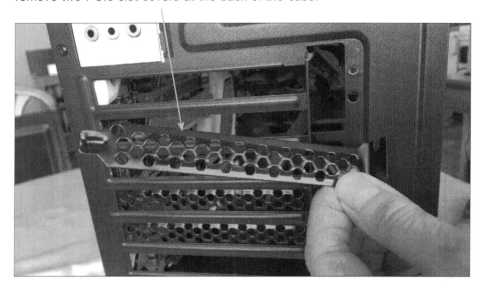

Manoeuvre the card into position over one of the PCIe x16 slots, making sure its cut-out is aligned with the lug in the slot.

When doing this, hold the card by the edges so your fingers don't come into contact with the circuitry.

...cont'd

Push the card into the slot until the retaining clip closes. Make sure you press evenly on both ends so the clip doesn't engage before the card is fully inserted. Otherwise, you may end up with it being stuck half in and half out. If this happens, it can be difficult to remove the card so you can try again.

Secure the card with one of the screws taken from the slot covers.

Power Supply Unit

Installing the PSU is straightforward enough. Connecting the cables to the system requires a bit more thought, though. Proceed as follows:

Slide the PSU into position. In most system cases these days, this is at the bottom of the case. Secure the PSU with the supplied screws.

...cont'd

Now locate the power sockets for the motherboard and CPU, and plug in the respective PSU connectors.

Motherboard and CPU power cables connected..

SATA Drives

Most system cases come with a dedicated bay in which to install the various types of drive. The actual method of securing them varies from case to case. In some, they simply screw in place while in others they are mounted on a removable tray that screws or clips into place.

In our case, there are two bays - one for traditional HDDs and one for SSDs. Below, we show the HDD being installed:

The drive being placed in the bay and screwed into place.

...cont'd

The next step is to plug a SATA power cable into the drive.

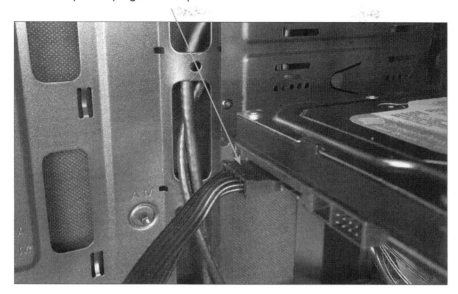

And then a SATA interface cable.

Finish by connecting the other end of the interface cable to a SATA port on the motherboard.

The procedure for installing a SSD is exactly the same.

Case Connections

With all the components installed and connected to the motherboard, the last step is hooking up the case connections. These include the power and reset switches, power LED, HDD indicator LED, front panel USB and audio sockets, and case fans. Some systems may also have RGB lighting, a case speaker, thermal sensor, chassis intrusion sensor, and more.

System panel connections are in a header bank that is usually located at the bottom-right of the motherboard.

Front panel USB connection. The motherboard will also provide USB headers for connecting additional USB modules.

Front panel audio socket connection.

Take particular care when connecting the power switch. The pins in the system panel header bank are very small and close together. Study the motherboard manual to make sure you get it right, otherwise you will be greeted by a blank screen when you switch on for the first time. Connecting it to the wrong pins is one of the most common mistakes made by system-builders.

CHAPTER 11

Getting the System Operational

Operating Systems

With your gaming machine's hardware taken of, it's now time to take a look at the software you intend to run on it. We'll start with the most important one of all - the operating system. Here, there are three options:

* Windows
* Mac OS x
* Linux

Windows

Over the years, the Windows operating system has been available in a number of versions, each by and large, an improvement on their predecessors. These have included Windows 95, 98, NT, 2000, XP, Vista, 7 and 8.

The latest version, Windows 10, is the most advanced and reliable yet. It has two huge advantages over the competition - it's sheer user-friendliness that makes it the easiest system to use, and the fact that literally all games, and virtually all software, work well on it.

Its only downside is that it does still have instability issues that are particularly noticeable when playing computer games.

Mac OS X

As with Windows, Mac OS X has been through a number of incarnations, the current one of which is Catalina. The beauty of this operating system is the high level of security it offers. Also, because it is optimised to work with Apple's hardware, it is far more efficient than either Windows 10 or Linux.

However, it can only be used on Apple computers. The operating system is not compatible with non-Apple hardware.

...cont'd

Linux

For most people investigating operating systems, Linux isn't the first name to spring to mind. Indeed, many people have never even heard of it. However, it is a perfectly capable system that is freely available for download to anyone who wants to give it a try.

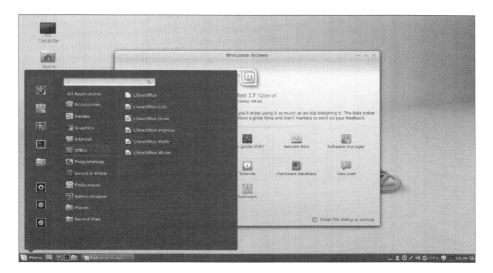

Linux is open-source and there are many different versions all running on the same basic architecture. Unlike OS X, it can be installed on any computer which overcomes the hardware limitation imposed by Macs. However, it is difficult to get to grips with and compatible software (including games) is not widely available.

Summary

Windows has to be the choice for a gaming computer. Virtually all games and other types of software are written specifically for it. Plus, of course, everyone knows how to use it.

OS X is restricted to Apple Macs which, in any case, have hardware limitations that make them totally unsuitable for anything but the most basic games.

Linux is also unsuitable for gaming for the simple fact very few games work with it. Plus, it's not a particularly intuitive operating system that most people who are brought up with Windows find difficult to use.

Create a Boot Disk

Assuming you have decided to go with Windows, you now need a way of installing it. This requires two things - Windows itself and a USB flash drive with a capacity of at least 8 GB. You need to create the boot disk beforehand on a different computer.

Helpfully, Microsoft has a boot disk creation tool on its website. Just type "Microsoft media creation tool" into your browser and follow the link to download it. Connect your USB drive and then run the media creation tool.

Click Accept at the terms and conditions screen and then at the next screen, select the "Create installation media ..." option.

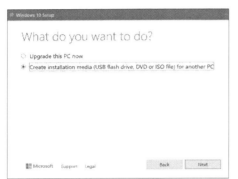 

At the next screen, click Next to open the "Choose which media to use" screen. Select the USB flash drive option and, at the following screen, select the USB drive you want to use. Then click Next to open the download screen.

 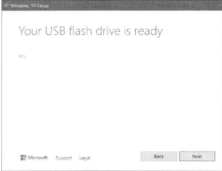

The tool will now download Windows 10 and create a boot disk on the USB drive. When done, disconnect the drive and put it somewhere safe.

Installing Windows

With your previously created boot disk, you are now ready to install Windows. Connect the disk to the computer and switch on. One of two things will happen: Either the PC will detect the boot disk automatically and tell you to press ... key to start the installation, or it will stop at the first boot screen as shown below.

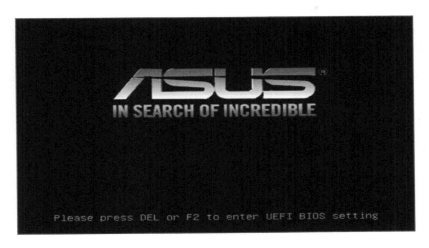

In the latter case, you need to tell the PC where to find the boot disk. Press the specified key to enter the BIOS - usually Delete or F2 - and locate the boot options. This will open in a new window that shows all the drives connected to the computer, including the Windows boot disk.

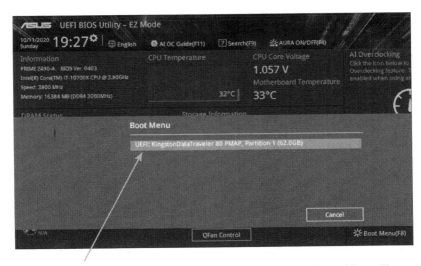

Click the boot disk to start the Windows installation procedure. You will now be taken out of the BIOS environment and Windows will begin loading its installation files from the disk.

Select the required language, and time and currency format, and then click Next. In the screen that opens, click the "Install Now" button

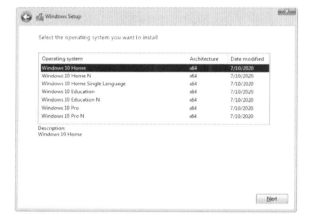

In the next screen enter the Windows product key and click Next.

Select the version of Windows to be installed

Accept the license terms

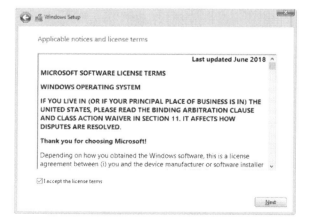

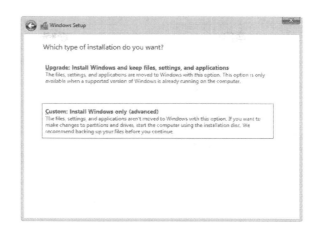

For the type of installation, select the "Custom:Install Windows only (advanced)" option

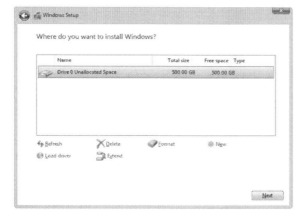

If you only have one drive in the PC, it will be selected automatically. Click Next.

However, if you have more than one drive, select the one you want as the boot drive

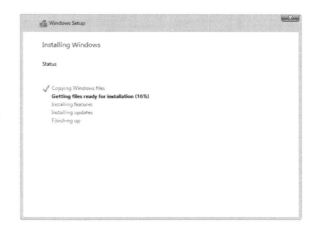

Click Next and Windows will install itself on the drive

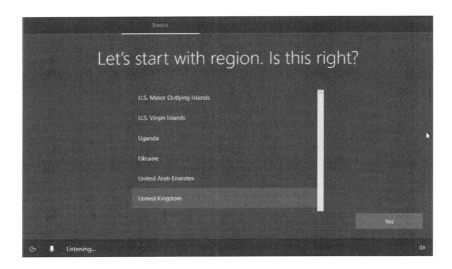

You'll now see a succession of setting up screens. These include region, keyboard layout, signing in to your Microsoft account (or creating one), creating a login pin, privacy settings, etc, etc.

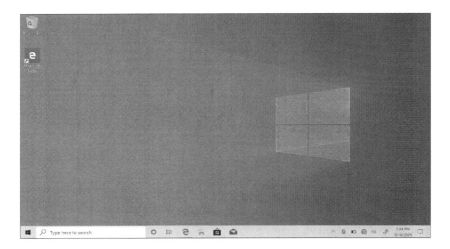

Eventually the installation will complete and you'll see the Windows desktop appear on your screen. On a well specified computer, it should take no longer than half an hour or so.

Assuming you are connected to the Internet, Windows will immediately check for updates and install any it finds. To do it manually, click the Start button and go to Settings > Update & Security > Windows Update. Once that has been done, your Windows installation is ready to use.

BIOS Settings

With the operating system taken care of, the next stage involves the BIOS. Fortunately, this is not as big an issue as it used to be. Unless you intend to overclock your system (see Chapter 13), there's actually only one thing you need to change and another that's optional. We'll start with the latter.

Updating the BIOS

As with all software, the BIOS utility can be updated. However, our advice is to leave well alone, particularly if you're inexperienced. Firstly, if things go wrong, you could end up with a computer that refuses to start.

Secondly, there's little to be gained as any changes will be minor - adding support for a new CPU for example. You won't see any improvements in performance or added features. However, should you wish to do it for whatever reason, this is the time because updating the BIOS undoes any changes made prior to the update.

Go the motherboard manufacturer's website and locate the BIOS update file. Download it and then save it on a USB flash drive. Make a note of the file's name as this will make it easier to locate when in the BIOS.

Reboot, enter the BIOS and open its Flash utility.

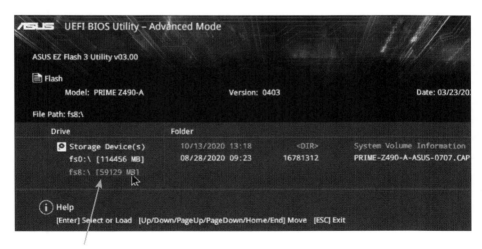

Under Storage Devices, you will see a list of all the drives in the computer. and, under Folder, the contents of the drives. Locate the USB drive containing the update file and then click the file in the Folder section.

A new window will open and you will be asked if you want to proceed with the update. Click Yes and the update will be installed.

...cont'd

Enable XMP or AMP

On page 48, we explained that memory modules are sold at a safe speed that's lower than their maximum. This is to help prevent system builders experiencing problems when getting their system set up.

So, when you have installed Windows, this needs to be changed. To do it, start the computer and enter the BIOS by pressing the required key. Then find the XMP or AMP setting.

Simply click to enable it. If you see more than one option, i.e. Profile 1 and Profile 2, start with the former. This will be the less extreme of the two settings. Save the change and exit the BIOS. To check the change has taken effect, re-enter the BIOS and look in the Hardware Monitor section.

This should show the memory running at its maximum speed (3000 MHz in our PC). Run the PC for a while and if you don't experience any problems, you can try enabling profile 2.

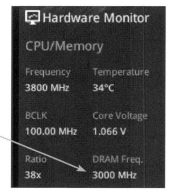

Installing Hardware Drivers

To complete the setting up of your new gaming machine, you now need to download and install the drivers for all hardware devices in your system. The only exception to this is the CPU, which doesn't require one. Don't forget the peripherals, such as the mouse, keyboard, game controllers, etc.

We suggest you start with the motherboard. With most of these boards, when you run Windows for the first time, you will be prompted to download a software utility that will locate and install all the necessary drivers for you. A typical example is the Armoury Crate utility from ASUS.

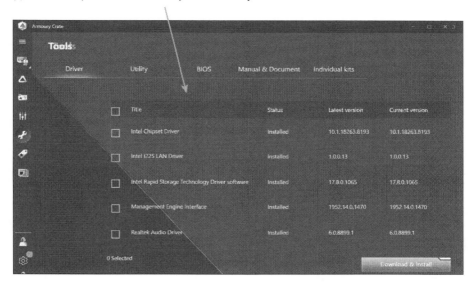

Many motherboards will provide a USB flash drive that contains the drivers. Our advice is to not bother with these as they are invariable out of date. Instead, use the download utility or go to the manufacturer's website and download the latest versions. Whichever way you get them, when they've been installed, you will be asked to reboot to complete the installation.

The same applies to your computer's graphics. Both Nvidia and AMD provide utilities (Geforce Experience and Radeon Adrenalin, respectively) that will download and install the graphics driver.

Then you need to visit the manufacturer websites to get the latest drivers for all the other hardware devices in your system.

One word of warning regarding these driver update utilities is that some will try to get you to install 3rd party applications. Typical examples of this are web browsers and anti-virus programs. So check which boxes are ticked before you click the Install button.

Benchmarking the System

You've installed Windows, hardware drivers and your applications. At this point, your gaming rig is optimally set up and running as well as it ever will. This, therefore, is the time to benchmark it and keep the results as a reference with which to compare future benchmarks. Doing so will enable you to monitor your rig's performance going forward and identify any of its components that are under-performing.

We suggest you do it with UserBenchmark. This analyses your PC and rates its major components. Also, because millions of people use UserBenchmark, you will be able to compare your system against others of similar or identical specifications. Save the result and use it to compare future tests.

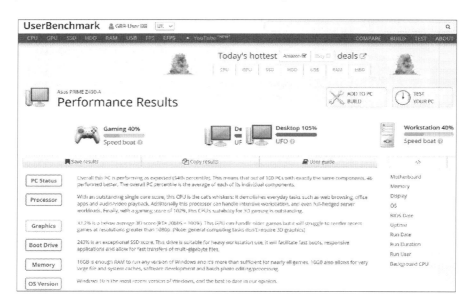

It's also possible to benchmark individual components to a much greater level. Here, we are talking about the ones that have the greatest impact on a PCs performance - the CPU, graphics card and system drive. One of the best for CPUs is Geekbench. Try Heaven UNIGINE for your graphics card and CrystalDiskMark for your drives.

Note that the above utilities provide what's known as "synthetic" benchmarks, i.e. they work on averages and so only give a general idea of performance. Another, perhaps more useful, method for gamers is Game Benchmarking. This works courtesy of benchmarks that are built-in to many games, and it gives you a real-world view of how your PC is functioning in an actual game. It's also useful when overclocking and/or adjusting game settings as it lets you see the effect of the changes in real time.

Useful Software

It's fairly safe to assume that your gaming computer won't be used exclusively for gaming. You'll also use it to browse the Internet and run other types of application. We're not going to make any suggestions here - you know what you need. What we *are* going to do is recommend some programs that you will find useful when in gaming mode.

Afterburner

Afterburner is a free graphics utility that provides a host of functions including overclocking, video capture, benchmarking and performance monitoring.

With regard to the latter, it shows the graphics card's clock speed, memory speed, voltage, fan speed and temperature in real time while playing games. Any adjustments made by the player can be saved as profiles and quickly switched between with hot-keys.

Razer Cortex

This is an optimisation utility from Razer. It has three sections:

The first is Game Booster, the purpose of which is to free up system resources when playing games. It does this by closing background applications, thus making more of the PC's resources available to the game.

System Booster removes junk files, clears browser history, optimises system configurations and defragments games. The latter function helps to speed up game loading time (note this only works on HDDs - SSDs are not supported).

Game Deals, as the name suggests, shows you the latest game deals from a variety of game-related websites.

Our only reservation with Razer Cortex concerns the Game Booster function. In our opinion, it doesn't have much effect as background applications on modern PCs don't use much in the way of resources. That apart, and considering it's free, we think it's a handy utility that's worth having.

CCleaner

CCleaner is a very popular system optimisation utility, and for good reason. It provides numerous tools and functions that will help keep your system in good shape.

These include a startup program manager that lets you choose which programs start with Windows, a Registry cleaner, a program uninstaller, a program updater, a drive analyser that shows you what types of files are occupying the drive (and how much space they are using), and a duplicate finder that locates duplicate files and lets you delete them.

Opera GX

Opera GX is a version of the Opera browser optimised for gamers. Not only does it look the part, it comes with features that include a customisable interface, system resource optimiser and a game volume control.

Another feature is GX Corner, which shows the latest games from the likes of Humble Bundle, and provides news streams pulled from various gaming sites.

Speccy

Speccy is a useful utility that provides an in-depth report of all the hardware in your system.

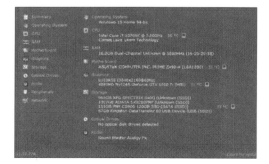

Very useful for gamers is its temperature monitoring feature that allows you to instantly check all your devices from one location.

It can also take snapshots and save them to a file. This can be extremely handy when making changes to the system's hardware and/or software.

CHAPTER 12

Peripherals

Gaming Mice

Gaming mice may bear a superficial resemblance to the bog-standard mice in general use but, under the hood, they are almost a different animal. Let's take a look at the features and specifications that make them so different, and factors you need to consider when buying one of these devices.

Purpose

If you play games of different types and need a mouse versatile enough to handle them all, an all-purpose gaming mouse will be the type to go for. However, if you play specific genres, such as MOBA, RTS, RPGs, etc, you will definitely need a more specialised mouse.

For example, RTS and MMO gamers will require extra buttons that can be mapped to specific functions, while FPS gamers will want a mouse capable of high accuracy and quick tracking.

Most game genres have mice built specifically for them. This simplifies buying one enormously.

Buttons

For everyday computer applications, a two-button mouse is quite adequate. Gamers, on the other hand, who need to activate a range of functions as quickly as possibly, need considerably more.

To this end, good gaming mice will provide at least six buttons which can be allocated to specific tasks. The Logitech G600 MMO, for example, comes with no less than twenty of them. With regard to how many *you* need, it basically comes down to the types of game you play.

Dots Per Inch (DPI)

DPI is the measure of how sensitive a mouse is to movement. The higher the DPI rating, the further the cursor will move for a given movement of the mouse.

While it is an important specification, it isn't as important as the manufacturers would have you believe. Games simply do not need extremely high levels of sensitivity (with the possible exception of multi-monitor gaming) and will respond perfectly well with a DPI of between 400 and 1200. As long as your chosen mouse is capable of this, you're covered.

A useful feature found on some gaming mice is a DPI switch that lets the gamer change DPI on-the-fly.

Sensor

Sensors come in two types - laser and optical. There is a lot of debate about which one is best, a big factor here being the issue of lag found in laser sensors. While there used to be some truth in this, laser technology has improved to the degree that laser lag is now rarely a problem.

Another bone of contention with laser mice is that of acceleration. This is caused by the LED picking up more information from the surface than the system can analyze, thus sending the tracking haywire. However, reducing the mouse's DPI setting is usually enough to eliminate the acceleration.

In all other respects, there is little to choose between the two types of sensor and the gamer will be well served by either.

Weight

Those of you who take gaming seriously may want to consider the weight of your mouse. This is a factor that can influence how you play as it effects the speed at which the mouse can be moved, and the accuracy with which the cursor can be positioned. Plus, of course, long sessions can be tiring on the hands and wrists.

With this in mind, top-end gaming mice are supplied with removable weights that let you make weight adjustments so they are not just more comfortable to use, but also more effective.

Wireless v Wired

Not so long ago this was a no-brainer. Wireless mice were simply incapable of the responsiveness needed for high speed games. That's no longer the case, however. Top-end models (and we stress top-end) are now a match for their wired cousins.

Anything less than top-end though, will suffer from lag to some degree. Wireless mice also rely on battery power. Their only real advantage is the lack of a cable which can interfere with movement.

Wired mice are more stable, generally more responsive and have the added bonus of costing less.

Gaming Keyboards

Choosing parts for a gaming PC is generally a numbers game - usually the higher the better. Gaming keyboards, though, introduce a different set of metrics and terminology as we'll see.

Switch Type

There are two types of keyboard - membrane and mechanical. The terms refer to the technology used in activating the keys. The former uses a layer of membrane which is covered by rubber domes, one under each key. With the latter, each key has its own spring-loaded mechanical switch.

Of the two, mechanical keyboards are the clear winners. Their key action is smooth and tactile, they are easier to clean as the key caps can be removed, and they are more durable and long lasting. Their drawbacks are the cost - they are considerably more expensive, and the fact they are noisier.

Note that mechanical keyboards are available with different types of switch, each having their own characteristics. You can choose between keys that are tactile (clicky) or linear (no click), keys with different distances of travel and keys with different actuation force. Many manufacturers, such as Razer and Logitech, grade the various types of mechanical switch by colour.

This issue of key type is one that professional gamers take very seriously.

Keyboard Size

Keyboards come in three sizes - full, compact and 60%. Full-size models include a full QWERTY alphanumeric section, a dedicated number pad, function keys and four directional cursor keys.

Compact keyboards leave out the number pad and, for this reason, are also known as "tenkeyless, or TKL" keyboards.

With 60% keyboards, all the function keys, and everything to the right of the Enter key are removed. This makes them the most compact type.

With most games, there is no benefit to having a number pad and so compact and 60% keyboards will fit the bill. Plus, of course, they have a smaller footprint which will be a consideration for some people. Another advantage is the ability to position the hands more closely when using the keyboard and mouse at the same time.

However, if you will be using the gaming rig for other types of application, or playing games that need a number pad, go for a full-size keyboard.

Macro Keys

Macro keys are dedicated function keys that, together with the appropriate software, enable you to create custom macros that activate a complex sequence of keystrokes and mouse clicks with just one keystroke. With games that require a rapid response, they are invaluable.

Top-end gaming keyboards let the gamer create profiles for specific games with the macro keys. This can be a big time-saver.

Ascetics

Computer gaming is not just about raw power and stunning frame rates. Many gamers want their system to look the part as well, and the keyboard is no exception to this.

Low-end keyboards have a single back-light under the keys, but high-end models use RGB lighting in each key. Many of these come with software that lets the gamer create custom lighting patterns.

Visually stunning as they are, these lights serve another purpose by enabling the gamer to divide the keyboard into specific zones that are identifiable by colour. This facilitates gameplay by providing a quick visual reference to required keys.

Wireless v Wired

The situation with regard to connectivity is much the same as it is with gaming mice. While wireless keyboards are convenient and help to reduce clutter, they are prone to lag. It's only top-end (and very expensive) wireless keyboards that are on a par with wired keyboards in this respect.

So unless, you are prepared to pay a premium price, a wired keyboard is the recommended option.

Game Controllers

Many gamers swear by their keyboards and mice and see no need to use anything else. And for strategy games, shoot-em-ups, MOBAs and MMOs, we don't necessarily disagree. But it is a fact that some people find it easier to play these games with a controller and that for some game genres, a dedicated controller is well nigh essential.

Game controllers are available in three types: gamepads, joysticks and racing wheels. The following are all factors that need to taken into account when buying one of these devices:

Wireless v Wired

As with other types of peripheral, game controllers that connect via a cable are the preferred option for optimum performance. Wireless connections are not quite as good.

Range

A big drawback with a wired controller is its range - typically 6 to 9 feet. Wireless models, on the other hand, have a range of up to 30 feet which allows the gamer to sit much further back from the screen.

Power

Wireless controllers rely on battery power - their wired cousins, of course, are powered by the computer. So if you are the type of gamer who plays for hours on end and want to use a wireless model, this is an important consideration. Go for one that offers a long playing time between battery changes. Controllers that do will be at the top (and expensive) end of the market.

Comfort

Given you'll be holding your controller for long periods, it's essential that it's comfortable. Weight, layout and grip are all factors in this regard. We highly recommend buying from a store where you can try before you buy, rather than taking a chance online.

Build Quality

Another advantage of trying before buying is that you can assess the build quality. Quite apart from the risk of being dropped, spillages, etc, emotions can run high when playing and result in the controller being hurled across the room in disgust, or similar. So if you have to buy online, stick with a reputable manufacturer, such as Microsoft, Logitech, Razer, Steel Series, etc.

Features

Game controllers come with a range of features. Programmable buttons, under buttons, touchpads, rear inputs, adjustable triggers and magnetic charging docks are just some. One very important feature that your controller really should have is a vibration system that adds an element of realism to games.

Some controller-specific features are:

Racing Wheels

Probably the most important feature a racing wheel should have is force feedback from a vibration system. This helps the driver determine exactly when to brake, accelerate and turn corners. Plus, of course, feeling the inevitable crash.

A separate gearstick and pedals is highly recommended and makes for a much more realistic driving experience. Not all wheels have this so check it out in the specifications.

Racing wheels have specific rotation angles, i.e. the amount of turn in the wheel before it locks. With some, it's adjustable while with others it's fixed. The higher the angle, and thus more turn, the better.

Joysticks

Good joysticks come with a throttle that provides more precise control over speed. With cheaper models, this is incorporated into the stick which is not ideal. The best quality joysticks, on the other hand, provide a separate throttle which is much easier to use.

Low-end joysticks only offer X- and Y-axis control, i.e. forward, back, left and right. For many games this is perfectly adequate. However, joysticks that also offer Z-axis control take things to a different level by making it possible to control 3D movement by twisting the stick clockwise or anticlockwise. This feature replicates an aircraft's rudder controls.

As a final note, while making sure your chosen controller offers everything needed for the games you play, take care to avoid having *too* many features and controls. These can be confusing and may be more of a hindrance than anything else.

Headsets

Although their sound quality is not as good as that of headphones, headsets excel in other ways that only gamers will appreciate. Important considerations here include:

Surround Sound

Surround sound creates the illusion of being in the middle of the action, literally. If something moves behind you, you'll know it's behind you. Of the various standards, Dolby 7.1 is the best followed by 5.1.

However, the higher the standard used, the more expensive the headset. So to make surround sound worthwhile, the games you play need to benefit from it. For example, FPS games like Overwatch, Battlefield and Call of Duty all play better with 7.1. With MOBA games, such as League of Legends and virtually all single player games, 5.1 and even stereo is quite adequate.

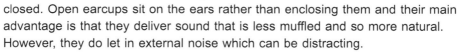

Open or Closed Earcups

Earcups are the part of the headset that cover the ears and can be either open or closed. Open earcups sit on the ears rather than enclosing them and their main advantage is that they deliver sound that is less muffled and so more natural. However, they do let in external noise which can be distracting.

Closed earcups encase the ears completely, thus blocking out most external sound. With less distraction, the gamer is better able to concentrate. This is the best option for playing in noisy environments.

Noise Cancellation

Niose cancellation is a very useful feature that is restricted to headsets with a boom microphone. With these, the microphone inverts external sounds and effectively cancels them. While not perfect, the technology is effective enough to block most noise. As with closed earcup headsets, it is useful as an aid to concentration.

Microphone

Headset microphones are either built-in or attached to a boom. While the former are more comfortable in use, boom mics are the better option. Not only is their audio quality superior, they provide noise cancellation as described above. Uni-directional microphones are better than omni-directional models as they don't pick up off-axis sounds. This makes for clearer game chat.

Speakers

Most gamers prioritise graphics over sound. In our opinion, this is a mistake as the better the sound quality, the better and more enjoyable gaming will be. For those not in the know, the following are the important factors:

Channels

Speaker systems come in 2.0, 2.1, 5.1, 6.1 and 7.1 configurations. The first figure specifies the number of speakers and the second figure specifies the number of subwoofers. The latter improve bass levels and add depth, dynamism and a sense of spaciousness to the audio.

Gaming speakers mostly come in 2.0 and 2.1 setups and, for the vast majority of gamers, these will be perfectly adequate. Top-end systems have 5.1 channels and utilise surround sound technology that allows the player to detect by sound as well as by sight. They also offer the added option of being able to relax to some nice music when you've run out of opponents to slaughter!

Output Power

Rated in watts, a speaker system's output power is a determining factor in its maximum volume level. For most gamers, a 40 watt system will be fine. Top-end 5.1 systems can be as high as 400 watts.

Note that output power is not indicative of sound quality. For this, you need to consider specifications such as frequency response, impedance and sensitivity. Another factor here is the sound system in the computer. Integrated systems and low quality sound cards will not produce top quality audio no matter how good the speakers are.

Connectivity

Most speakers connect to the PC via a 3.5 mm jack or by Bluetooth. The latter is particularly suitable for multi-speaker setups as it eliminates the mess of connecting cables.

Another type of connection found on some top-end speakers is TOSLINK. This is an optical connection more commonly used with professional audio systems.

Features

Cheap speakers provide little, or nothing, in the way of control. At the minimum, your speakers should have volume, bass and treble controls. A remote control will be even better.

Microphones

Good as the boom microphones on gaming headsets can be, they aren't a patch on a dedicated microphone. As you fondly imagine yourself bellowing aggressively at opponents in the battlefield, they will probably only hear a weak, tinny voice that denotes nothing but weakness. So, to ensure you sound the part, as well as looking it, a dedicated mic is much the better option. Check the following before buying one:

Polar Pattern

A microphone's polar pattern is a specific section of the area surrounding it from which it will pick up sound. For example, a microphone with a cardoid polar pattern is most sensitive at the front and least sensitive at the back.

Good quality gaming microphones can be switched between stereo, omnidirectional, bidirectional, cardioid and polar patterns, whereas low-end mics may only offer one. Note that some patterns are better for certain games.

Frequency Response

This is an important specification that indicates the lowest and highest pitched sounds the microphone is capable of picking up. It should be between 20 Hz and 20 KHz for the simple reason these are the limits of human hearing.

High quality mics go beyond these limits. As a result, they detect sub-harmonic detail that gives them extra clarity.

Inline Monitoring

Inline monitoring lets you hear your voice through a pair of headphones as you speak, thus making life easier for those on the receiving end - people invariably speak too loudly if they can't hear themselves. To facilitate this, some microphones provide a headphone jack. It's well worth having in team games.

Features

Controls to alter the volume and mix are useful, as is a mute button that will temporarily deactivate the microphone thus allowing you to cut out unwanted sounds. Also useful is an adjustable stand that lets you alter the angle of the mic. Some mics can be fitted to a boom arm if a stand isn't required.

Finally, mics that have a metal mesh are much easier to clean than those with cloth mesh. The need to do this is inevitable with a well used mic.

Webcams

Virtually all laptops and all-in-one PCs these days come equipped with a webcam. Self-built PCs, however, do not (unless the builder has had the foresight to buy a monitor with an integral webcam). Even if they have, it's an unfortunate fact that built-in webcams are almost always of a very low quality.

So, if you want a decent model for your gaming, you're going to have to buy one separately. Check them out as follows:

Resolution
The higher a webcam's resolution, the sharper the video it produces. Many webcams are only 720p and are the minimum you should consider. The video will be grainy but passable. If you want clear, vibrant, video, look for a resolution of 1080p. For the very best quality, 4K is the way to go.

Frame Rate (FPS)
A high frame rate is also essential for video quality. If it's too low, the video will be slow and jerky and may periodically freeze. This specification is measured in frames per second and 30 FPS is the minimum you should accept. The best webcams have a FPS of 60.

Field of View (FOV)
Field of view (also known as viewing angle) is the area that a camera can see. It is measured in degrees and the wider the FOV, the more the camera will capture.

Most webcams have a FOV of around 75, which is fine for most purposes. For gaming though, our recommendation is to go with a FOV of at least 100. Just remember, the wider FOV, the greater the risk of image distortion

Autofocus
Webcams come with two types of focus - fixed and automatic. Low-cost cameras employ the fixed focus method in which the lenses don't move and so can only capture images clearly within a specified range of distances. Anything out of that range will be blurred.

Better quality webcams use automatic focussing. This adjusts the lenses so that the subject is always kept in focus.

Routers

Your broadband router may not be the first thing to spring to mind when planning a gaming PC. But if you're into online gaming and want the fastest and most reliable connection, you should be aware that standard home routers will not deliver the best performance possible. This means you need to investigate the burgeoning gaming router market. Thanks to the ever increasing popularity of online gaming, most of the router manufacturers are now offering models designed specifically for this purpose.

Features you need to consider are:

Quality of Service (QOS)

This is the main difference between a gaming router and a standard router. The latter treats all traffic, regardless of type (uploading/downloading, internet browsing, streaming, gaming, etc), equally by giving them the same level of priority.

So, if you're playing a game at the same time someone else in the house is streaming a movie, unless you have super-fast broadband, your gameplay may be adversely affected.

QoS ensures your game is given priority over all other types of traffic. Different manufacturers have their own versions of QoS; Qualcomm's StreamBoost for example.

Ethernet Ports

Gamers who use multiple devices simultaneously, or don't want to be constantly connecting and disconnecting devices, should look at the number of Ethernet (LAN) ports the router provides. Gaming routers provide up to ten of these.

Currently, the fastest Ethernet standard is 10 Gigabit and is supported by many top-end gaming routers. However, speeds of this magnitude are only needed in server setups - the only reason a gamer might want it is for future-proofing.

Wi-Fi 6 Support

For the fastest and most reliable connection, Ethernet is the best option. Should you need a wireless connection though, the best performance will be provided by the latest Wi-Fi 6 standard. High-end gaming routers are powerful enough to deliver fast Wi-Fi to every corner of the house - something standard routers cannot do.

Virtual Reality Systems

We touched on Virtual Reality on page 56. Here, we'll take a closer look. VR is currently one of the hottest topics in the gaming world. Not just gaming either in fact, as evidenced by Facebook buying out a leading VR company, Oculus Rift, seeing it as a potentially new type of communication medium.

What is Virtual Reality?

The clue is in the name - it's a virtual, computer-generated, 3D world in which players interact by means of a head-mounted display and various types of input tracking. VR makes the player feel as though he/she is really there, both mentally and physically.

There are several variations of VR which include collaborative, fully-immersive, non-immersive, and web-based. The fully-immersive variation is the one currently taking the gaming world by storm and so is the one we look at here.

Requirements for VR

To enter a virtual world, you need four things: a headset that lets you see the world, an input tracking device that lets you interact with it and a computer or console to power it. Plus, of course, a VR game that generates the world.

The Oculus Quest, shown opposite, is the exception, being an all-in-one VR platform with its own built-in hardware that includes a CPU and graphics system. It's a brilliant device for less demanding VR games but struggles with games like Half Life Alyx.

However, this limitation can be overcome by connecting it to a computer via a fibre-optic cable. This lets it harness the extra power needed for more demanding games.

VR headsets work by means of motion detecting sensors that track the wearer's head movements. Turn your head to the right and you will look to the right in the game, tilt your head up and you will look up. Stereoscopic 3D adds another dimension.

The setup is completed by motion detecting controllers that project hand and finger movements into the virtual world. The fact that physical movements are mirrored in the game adds to the sense of immersion.

These controllers (one for each hand) have buttons on the top and triggers underneath for the index and middle fingers, plus a thumb-controlled joystick. They essentially give the player virtual hands which can do everything a real hand can do - close into a fist, point, grab, throw things, pick up objects, etc, etc.

For all this to happen, of course, the VR system needs processing power. Just how much depends on the game but the following is a good guide:

Minimum	Maximum
Intel Core i5 or AMD Ryzen 5 CPU	Intel Core i7 or AMD Ryzen 7 CPU
Graphics card with 4 GB onboard memory	Graphics card with 6 GB onboard memory
8 GB system memory	16 GB system memory

Many graphics card manufacturers now make cards that are compatible with virtual reality. Look for "VR Ready" in the specifications.

The final piece in the VR jigsaw is the software. Although we are looking at VR through the prism of gaming here, there are many other potential uses for the technology, such as sport, medical training and education.

Not surprisingly, most games that support VR are of the first person variety. The technology is particularly effective in racing games and flight simulators. Some VR games are existing titles that have been updated to work with the new medium, e.g. The Elder Scrolls V. These are ideal as a learning experience for those dipping their toes into the VR world for the first time (it does take some getting used to).

Then there are games developed specifically for VR. Good examples here are Iron Man VR and Beat Saber. Players experienced with VR will be right at home with these.

Also available are multi-player VR games. Challenge your opponents in games such as Star Trek: Bridge Crew, No Man's Sky VR, Payday 2: VR, Arizona Sunshine and Echo VR. You may enjoy the experience so much you might never go back to non-VR gaming.

CHAPTER 13

Overclocking

Introduction

This chapter is for gamers who want to get the best possible performance from their new machine. To do it, they need to change the factory settings of three components - the CPU, graphics card and system memory. The process of doing this is known as overclocking.

What Does Overclocking Do?

Overclocking increases a component's clock speed so that it runs faster than it was designed to. As a result, it will carry out more operations per second, thus boosting performance.

However, increasing a component's clock speed has knock-on effects. Firstly, the extra speed will require more power from the PSU. If the PSU can't supply it, a more powerful model will have to be installed.

Secondly, the extra power being used will result in more heat being generated. This may mean the component's cooling system, and possibly the case fans, having to be upgraded as well.

Can it be Overclocked?

All graphics cards and memory modules can be overclocked; the only question is to what degree. The situation with regard to CPUs is different though. If you are buying AMD, there's no problem - all recent AMD CPUs are overclockable.

However, this is not the case with Intel CPUs. If you are building an Intel system and want to overclock the CPU, you must make sure it's an unlocked model. These are signified by the letter K at the end of the CPU's name. For example, "Intel CORE I5-9600K".

Risks of Overclocking

CPUs, graphics cards and memory are built to operate within specific tolerances for reliability and longevity purposes. Going beyond those tolerances can damage them, even if they are designed to be overclocked. This means you risk voiding the guarantee. Even if you manage to overclock without causing damage, you may end up with an unstable system that is prone to errors. This is manageable though and can be fixed by going back into the settings and lowering them as necessary.

Be aware that cooling systems bundled with CPUs are not suitable for use with overclocked CPUs. Use a good quality air cooler or a liquid cooling system.

Anyone planning to overclock an Intel CPU may be interested to know that this manufacturer is selling "performance tuning protection plans" for certain of their processors. These expand the guarantee to cover damage due to overclocking.

Should You Overclock?

Overclocking a CPU can increase it's speed by up to 35 percent or so. With graphics cards and memory, 10 to 15 percent. On the face of it, these are worthwhile gains that must surely be worth the effort of doing it. Yes?

Well, no, not necessarily. It depends on what you use the computer for. While the speed of a CPU does affect gaming performance, it has much more of an effect on overall computer performance, and specific types of application such as video editing. With the vast majority of games, the difference made by a boost of, say, 25 percent, will hardly be noticeable. If you're editing a video, on the other hand, it most definitely will be.

It's with the graphics card and memory that overclocking provides the most benefit to the gamer and is well worth doing, the graphics card in particular. Having said all that, as an overclocked CPU will be of benefit in some games, and will boost overall system performance, it makes sense to do it anyway.

What's Needed?

With regards the CPU, it must be an unlocked model, as already mentioned. The motherboard must also support overclocking - not all do, so check the specifications.

You will also need overclocking software. All BIOS utilities provide an overclocking tool with a manual option (for doing it the hard way) and an automatic option (for doing it the easy way). Alternatively, AMD and Intel both provide a free utility that is designed to simplify the overclocking of their respective CPUs.

An important part of successful overclocking is keeping a very close eye on the effects of changed settings. This requires the use of monitoring software, a good example of which is CPU-Z.

To make sure your overclocked devices are stable, they must be stress-tested. Here, you will be using programs such as Prime95, LinX, and AIDA64. These are all free to download.

PLEASE NOTE

The descriptions and related pictures in this chapter of how to overclock are taken from the author's PC. In yours, they will probably be slightly different, as may the terminology used. However, as all BIOS utilities are much the same, the differences will be negligible and certainly not enough to cause any confusion.

Benchmarking

Benchmarking provides a way of evaluating not just the performance of a component after it has been upgraded or overclocked, but also how it performs in comparison to other components of the same type.

There are two types of benchmark - synthetic and real-world. The former is basically an evaluation of many different tasks, the figures for which are weighed and combined into a single score. With CPU's, these tasks include web browsing, file compression, floating-point calculations and rendering.

Popular synthetic benchmarking tools include 3DMark, Passmark, Intel Extreme Tuning Utility (shown below) and PCMark 10.

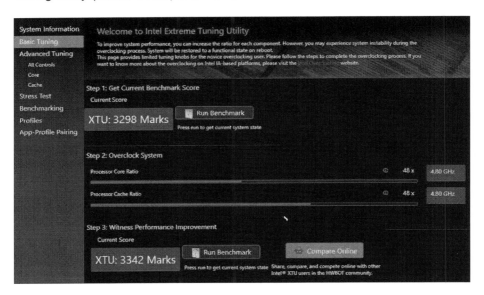

Real-world benchmarks, by contrast, employ commonly used applications such as Handbrake (video encoding) and 7-Zip (file compression). These give a more accurate indication of how the component will perform in a real-world scenario. For gamers, in-game benchmark tools are one type of real-world test.

Synthetic benchmarks provide the best option for a quick, general comparison, but real-world benchmarks are far more accurate, and thus more useful, for people building a PC with a specific purpose in mind, such as gaming.

With regard to the CPU, benchmark utilities usually show single-core and multi-core scores. Single-core scores are more relevant with lightly threaded games, and applications that only need a single core. However, for heavily threaded games that use several cores, the multi-core score is the figure to take note of.

CPU Overclocking Basics

Before getting into the mechanics of overclocking your CPU, we'll take a look at the basic principles, knowledge of which will help you to understand what you're doing and why.

As we've already seen, the speed of a CPU is set by its frequency, or clock speed. The higher this is, the faster the CPU can handle the millions of calculations needed for the system to run.

There are three factors that determine CPU clock speed:

* Base Clock Speed (BCLK) - this is the CPU's base frequency and is set at a safe level at which all the CPU's cores can run without any problems

* Multipliers (also known as core multipliers) - each of the CPU's cores has its own multiplier. These are applied to the base frequency and, together, they produce the CPU's operating frequency

* Voltage (Vcore) - this refers to the voltage that powers the CPU. The higher the frequency, the more voltage required by the CPU

Overclocking is essentially increasing the core multipliers, which in turn increase the CPU's frequency. For example, applying a core multiplier of 42 to a BCLK of 100 MHz, produces a frequency of 4200 MHz, or 4.2 GHz.

The key to overclocking successfully is raising the CPU's frequency incrementally in very small amounts and evaluating the result each time before repeating the process. It can't be stressed highly enough how important this is.

Eventually, a level will be reached beyond which it is impossible to go without experiencing stability issues. At this point, the system will be overclocked to its maximum.

Raising the frequency may also necessitate increasing the CPU's voltage, and quite possibly adjusting other performance-related settings as well, in order to keep the system stable.

Higher speeds and voltages result in more heat being generated, so it is essential that the CPU's cooling system is up to the job. Depending on your system and how high you want the overclock to go, you may need to water-cool the CPU.

An overclocked CPU will typically require about an extra 150 watts from the PSU. So before you start overclocking, make sure it has the spare capacity.

Automatic CPU Overclocking

There are two ways to overclock a CPU - manually and automatically. Here, we are going to look at the automatic method.

The UEFI BIOS utility in all modern motherboards provides an automatic over-clocking tool. This enables you to give your system a considerable boost with a single click of the mouse. However, bear in mind that these utilities tend to play it safe by not pushing the settings too high - this ensures the system is stable afterwards. If you're after the maximum overclock possible, you need to take the manual route.

To get going with your automatic overclock, start the PC and enter the BIOS. In our PC, the auto overclock feature (AI Overclocking) is on the opening screen:

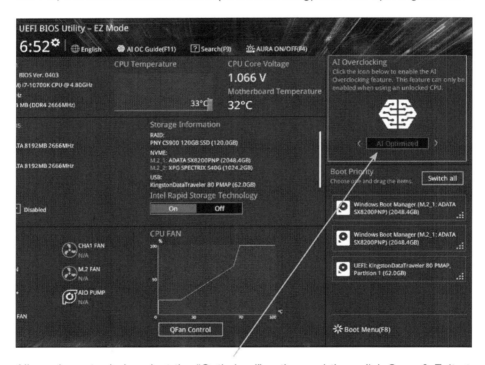

All you have to do is select the "Optimized" option and then click Save & Exit at the bottom-right of the screen. The computer will now reboot and on the splash screen you should see a message stating the CPU has been overclocked and by what percentage.

When back in Windows, stress-test the PC by playing a resource-intensive game for a while. In all likelihood, though, everything will be fine. As we said above, automatic over-clocking does not push the CPU to its limits. We'll see how to do that next.

Manual CPU Overclocking

The first step is to measure the baseline performance of your system with a benchmarking utility. This will give you a figure to compare the overclock with. Next, enter the BIOS and, on the opening screen, you should see the details of your current configuration. In the example below, the CPU has a speed of 3800 MHz, a temperature of 29 C and a core voltage of 1.066 volts.

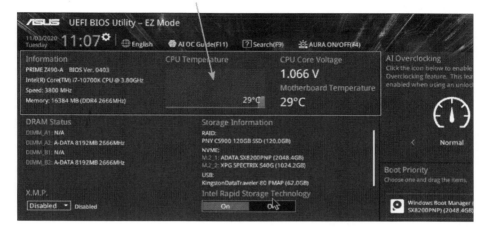

Click Advanced Mode at the bottom-right and in the next screen click AI Tweaker. This opens the manual overclock tool. At the right, you should see the current BCLK (the CPU's base clock speed), and the current Ratio (this is another word for multiplier).

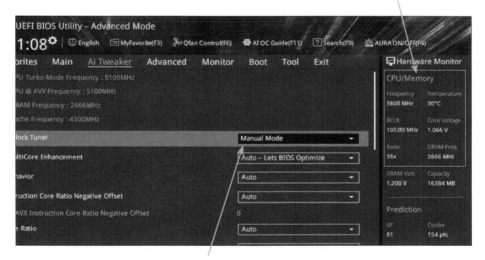

Because modern BIOS utilities have a range of auto settings, you may have to switch from Auto to Manual in order to access the multiplier settings. Do this in the drop-down menu alongside AI Overclock Tuner by selecting Manual Mode.

...cont'd

Now you should see the CPU Core Ratio setting appear. Click the drop-down box alongside and you'll see three options: Sync All Cores, By Core Usage and AI Optimized. The first two are the ones we're interested in.

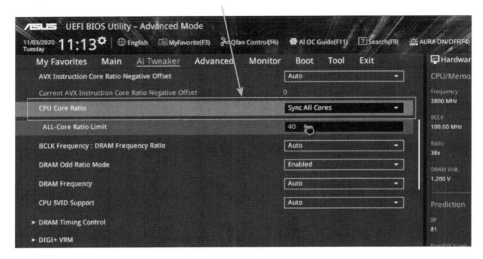

If you select Sync All Cores, as shown above, you'll see an All-Core Ratio Limit setting appear. Any value you type in the box will be applied to all the CPU's cores, i.e. you'll be increasing the multiplier on all of them simultaneously.

If you select By Core Usage, you'll see a Core Ratio Limit setting for each of the CPU's cores as shown below. This lets you change the multiplier on a core-by-core basis.

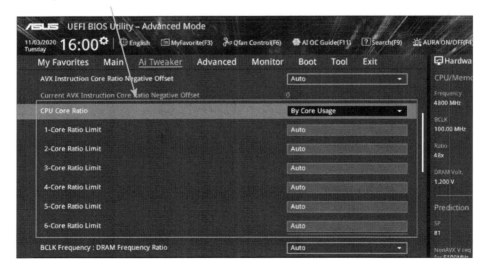

...cont'd

So, now that you know where to find the relevant settings, begin your overclock by raising the core multiplier (or multipliers) by a value of 1. Save the change and boot into Windows. Run your benchmark utility again and you should see the change reflected in a higher benchmark score. To make sure your overclock is stable, now run a stress test. If all appears to be well, you have successfully overclocked your CPU.

To achieve the maximum overclock possible, keep repeating the above procedure until the system fails. At this point, you need to raise the CPU's voltage incrementally until the system is OK again. To do this, go back into the overclock utility in the BIOS and scroll down the page until you see the CPU Core/Cache Voltage setting.

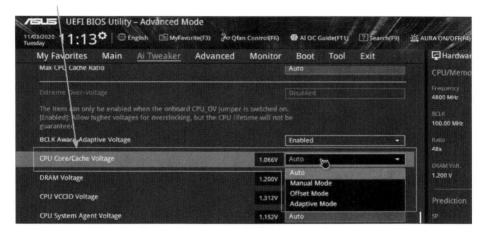

Click the drop-down menu and you'll see three alternative settings - Manual Mode, Offset Mode and Adaptive Mode.

Manual Mode is the simplest option - just type in the voltage you want and it will be applied regardless of whether the CPU is idling or heavily loaded. Offset Mode adds (or subtracts, if you wish to underclock) a set amount of power to the factory setting. This mode is more efficient as it lets the CPU's voltage vary according to its load while still being affected by the + or - change. In Adaptive Mode, the CPU's voltage will be increased only when it goes into Turbo Mode.

Don't raise the voltage by more than .0500 at a time. If several raises haven't had the desired effect, lower the multiplier. Achieving the right balance will be a question of trial and error and can take a very long time.

Don't forget to keep an eye on the CPU's temperature, particularly when stress-testing. Don't let it go above 90 degrees, otherwise you run the risk of the CPU failing prematurely. A monitoring utility such as CPU-Z is ideal for this.

Overclocking the Graphics Card

On page 137, we stated that an overclocked graphics card provides more of a performance boost in games than an overclocked CPU. The reason for this is that it handles far more of the huge amount of data involved in rendering video than the CPU does.

While largely the same, the process is rather easier than with CPUs and is done with a suitable overclocking utility from within Windows. There's no need to mess around in the BIOS at all.

Firstly, make sure you have the latest driver installed for your graphics card. It's not critical if you don't but, as the driver may well address issues that might affect the effectiveness of the overclock, it makes sense to do it. Next, you must benchmark the GPU. As with the CPU, make a note of the result so you have a comparison figure. Useful GPU benchmarking utilities include 3DMark, Passmark and FurMark.

When it come to the overclocking itself, you have a number of choices as to which utility to use. Our recommendation is MSI Afterburner, a free download from the MSI website. Fire it up and you'll see the following:

On the right, your GPU's current clock speed is displayed and, below, its memory clock speed. Dragging the scroll bar reveals more metrics. On the left are sliders that control the settings you need to adjust. These are:

* Core Voltage - this lets you adjust the voltage drawn by the GPU

...cont'd

- Power Limit - this lets you override the default limit that sets the power drawn from the PSU

- Core Clock - use this slider to specify the GPU's core clock speed

- Memory Clock - use this slider to specify the memory's clock speed

Below the sliders are three buttons: on the left is the Apply button, in the middle the Reset button, and on the right the Settings button.

Start the overclock by increasing the core clock speed - 10 MHz is enough - and click the Apply button. Now run your benchmark utility to confirm the change has taken effect. Then stress-test the card by either running a suitable

utility or playing a resource-intensive game for an hour or so. If you don't have any issues, you've successfully overclocked the card.

Now repeat the process, increasing the clock speed by 10 MHz each time until you start hitting problems. At this point, reduce the clock speed by about 20 MHz and apply the change. This is as far as you can take it for the time being.

Now turn your attention to the memory clock speed. Gradually adjust it by 50 MHz each time to the highest

setting you can. When you start getting problems, reduce the setting by about 100 MHz and apply the change.

By this stage, you should have achieved a good overclock. However, you can take it even higher by increasing the Core Voltage setting. This will need to be unlocked first though by clicking the Settings button and then checking the Unlock Voltage Control box. Then raise it by about 10 mV. With extra power now available, you should be able to increase both the clock and memory speeds even further. When you hit problems again, raise the voltage by another 10 mV and repeat until you can go no higher.

When raising the voltage, make sure you do not exceed the card's maximum limit. Also, keep an eye on the temperature and do not let it go above 90° C. If you do, you may be buying a new card sooner than you expected to.

Overclocking the Memory

The first thing to say with regard to overclocking memory is that the procedure is much safer than with the CPU and the graphics card. With both of these components, overclocking inevitably causes a rise in temperature and, if it goes too high, long-term damage may result. This is not a problem with memory, however, as memory modules do not generate anything like as much heat.

Memory performance depends primarily on two things: its frequency and its latency characteristics - the latter are often referred to as "timings". So to overclock memory, these two settings have to be adjusted.

Increasing its frequency will enable the memory to execute data transfers more rapidly. With the timings, however, lower is actually better. This is because each timing corresponds to a particular latency (the time between operations). The lower these latencies are, the better the memory's performance. Due to their dual role, changes in frequency will often require a counterbalancing change in the timings, and vice versa.

As always, before you start the overclock, establish a baseline level of performance with a benchmarking utility. Two that are suitable for this are Passmark and MaxxMEM2.

Then proceed as follows:

Open the BIOS overclock tool and scroll down past the CPU settings until you see the DRAM Frequency setting - this adjusts the memory's clock speed.

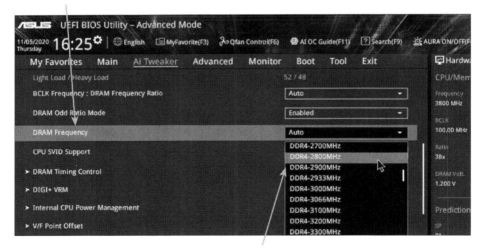

From the drop-down box, select the next highest frequency to the current one. Save the change, reboot and run a stress test. If the test is successful, keep raising the clock speed until the system becomes unstable. At this point, you'll

...cont'd

need to adjust the timings. To do this, click DRAM Timing Control - this opens a new page showing the timings settings.

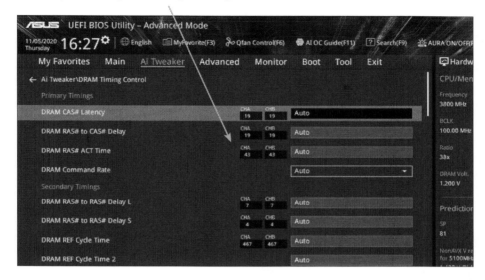

The ones you'll need to adjust are:

- DRAM CAS Latency (under Primary Timings)
- DRAM RAS to CAS Delay (under Primary Timings)
- DRAM RAS ACT Time (under Primary Timings)
- DRAM REF Cycle Time (under Secondary Timings)

Instead of increasing these timings as with most overclock settings, you will be decreasing them.

Reduce each timing by one value before rebooting into Windows to see what effect the changes have had. Repeat until the overclock is stable.

You can also see the memory timings in CPU-Z under the memory tab.

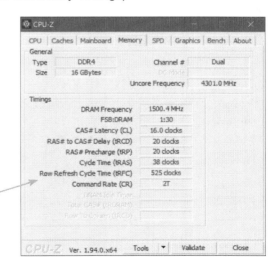

...cont'd

If you want to take the overclock even further, raise the memory's DRAM voltage setting and then repeat the overclock procedure. Be careful not to raise the voltage any higher than 1.4 volts, though.

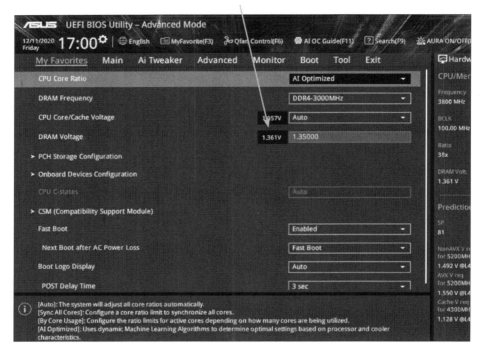

As with the CPU, overclocking memory manually is a fiddly procedure. For those who don't want the bother of it, there is always the automatic XMP option as we describe on page 116. Just remember the overclock won't be as high as can be achieved by doing it manually.

Overclocking used to be a dangerous activity as it, if taken too far, could easily damage components. These days, it's much safer as CPUs, GPUs and memory modules all have fail-safe mechanisms that kick in before any serious damage can be done. However, the risk of premature failure is still there.

Achieving a successful overclock manually is time consuming and the relatively small increase in performance may not be enough to make it worthwhile. For this reason, the automatic option may be your best bet. It's also the safest!

Before you can change settings in the BIOS, you first need to know the current default settings. Unfortunately, BIOS programs can be less than clear in this respect. Third-party utilities such as CPU-Z can help enormously here.

CHAPTER 14

Troubleshooting

The PC Won't Start

Problems with new builds are not unusual - we can testify to that from personal experience! Hopefully, you won't have any but you're on the right page if you do.

Power

Let's start with what's probably the most alarming issue of all - a PC that is seemingly stone dead when you press the power button. If you are unlucky enough to experience this, the following troubleshooting guide should get you out of trouble.

Firstly, make sure it really is dead. Remove the side panel and check there are lights on the motherboard and that the case fans are running. If there's neither, you have a power supply issue. Before condemning the PSU, check it's connection to the motherboard is secure. Then check it is switched on at the back and, finally, that there is power at the wall socket. If these three steps all check out, you have a faulty PSU. Replace it and go from there.

However, if the motherboard is lit and the case fans are active, the PC is very much alive - you just have to find out why it's playing dead. This brings us to a very common mistake made by self-builders - either they haven't connected the power switch, or have connected it to the wrong pins on the motherboard. These will be located on a bank of connectors on the right-hand side, or bottom-right, of the board.

The cable for the power switch is marked POWER SW on the connector. It doesn't matter which way round it is connected. This also applies to the reset switch (RESET SW).

...cont'd

Consult the motherboard manual and make sure it is connected correctly. It's very easy to get this wrong as, again, we can testify.

Monitor

Having established the motherboard is powered up and that the PC is switched on, the next thing to check is the monitor and its connection.

Firstly, make sure it is actually switched on - there will be a light somewhere on the case to indicate this. If it is, and assuming it is connected correctly, you should see the type of connection to the PC - DisplayPort or HDMI - displayed on the screen. If so, you know the monitor is working and is communicating with the PC.

If you don't, the monitor is either faulty or is not connected to the PC. If it's the latter, or there is no input from the PC, you will see a message on the screen to this effect. For example; "No Signal Source" or "No Input".

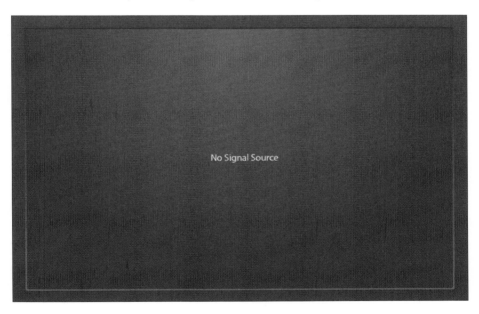

This is by far the most likely of the two scenarios and indicates either a bad connection or that the PC is faulty. Whichever, you will at least know the monitor itself is OK. If, after checking the connection to the PC is good, the message persists then the problem is with the graphics card, memory, CPU or motherboard.

Graphics Card

If your CPU has an integrated graphics system, uninstall the graphics card and connect the monitor to the integrated graphics output port. If you have something on the monitor now, either the graphics card is faulty or it wasn't connected properly.

Take it out and then refit it, making sure it clicks home firmly. These devices, particularly top-end models, are heavy and can pull out of the slot if not pushed right in. If you are still getting nothing, assume the graphics card is OK for the time being and move on.

Memory

The memory is the easiest component to check. It is also the least likely to be the cause of a blank screen, it has to be said.

Make sure all the modules are firmly seated in their slots and that the retaining clips are closed. If the computer still refuses to start, remove one of the modules and try again. Do this until you have checked all the modules individually. While it's possible one of them is faulty, it's almost impossible for them all to be.

If you're using just one large memory module, the last thing you can do is try it in a different slot in case the slot it's currently occupying is damaged or faulty.

CPU

The CPU is the next component to check. Start by making sure its power cable is connected. Assuming it is, remove the heatsink/fan assembly to gain access to the CPU. Then release the locking lever and check the device is correctly seated in its socket.

If it's not, in all likelihood, the pressure created by the locking lever will have bent some of its pins. You can try straightening them but, as they are so tiny, it's unlikely you'll be able to do it. In this situation, all you can do is swear long and loud, buy a new CPU and then make sure you fit it correctly at the second time of asking.

If it is correctly seated, however, refit the heatsink, not forgetting to wipe away the original thermal paste and replace it with some new paste.

Motherboard

Having checked everything else, you are now left with the motherboard. Take it out of the case and make sure there is nothing metal, such as a screw, on the board. This can cause a short circuit that prevents it from working. That done, turn it upside down and check for damage - this can be caused by scraping the board across the standoffs when installing it, for example.

If you don't see anything untoward, refit the motherboard making sure you use all the standoffs when screwing it down. Finally, rebuild the PC and try one last time. If it still doesn't start, you have to assume either the motherboard or the graphics card is faulty. Your only option now is to replace them, one at a time.

Instability Issues

Another common scenario with self-builds is that the system boots up, allowing you to install the operating system. Then you install the necessary drivers and start using the computer.

Except you can't because you keep running into instability issues. These can take various forms, such as the infamous Blue Screen of Death (BSoD).

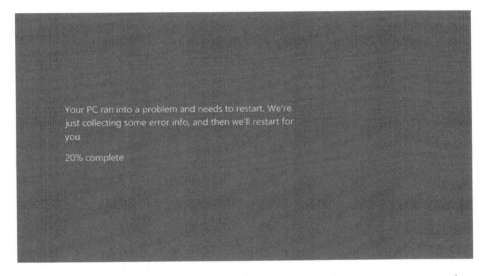

Your PC ran into a problem and needs to restart. We're just collecting some error info, and then we'll restart for you.

20% complete

This screen indicates that Windows has experienced a fatal system error and has crashed. The cause is often incompatible, or misconfigured, hardware and/ or hardware drivers. Very often, you'll experience random application crashes as well.

Assuming you've followed the advice in this book, it's unlikely to be hardware related so that leaves the drivers. Make sure you have installed the latest versions. If that doesn't help, the problem could be excess heat. If the PC runs for a short period and then crashes, the CPU could be overheating.

It could also be a build up of heat in the case. You can check this out on the Monitor page in the BIOS. This will show you the temperature of both the CPU

...cont'd

and the inside of the case as shown below.

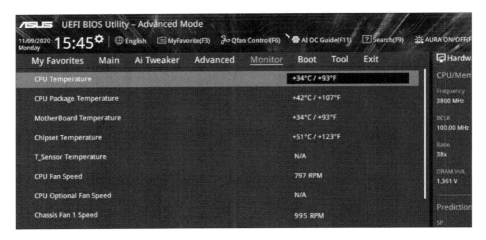

You can check the case fans are running from the BIOS as well and, if necessary, increase their speed using the Q-Fan Control utility.

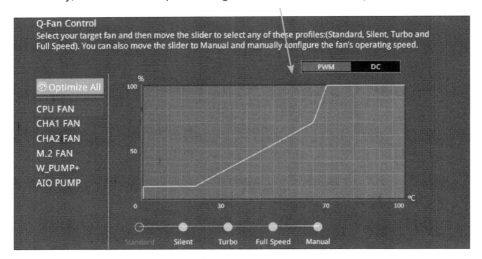

An overheating, or under-powered, PSU can also be the cause of an unstable computer. Again, check the PSU's fan is running and make sure its power rating is adequate for the hardware in the system.

Another potential cause of instability is the graphics card. Check it out as described on pages 151-152.

CHAPTER 15

Gaming Resources

Steam

With over 150 million users, Steam is probably the most important platform in the world of PC gaming. It's basically a marketplace where games can bought, sold and stored online. It also allows users to trade items, watch demos of upcoming games, and interact with the gaming community with features like in-game voice and chat functionality.

Steam hosts thousands of games, ranging from simple arcade games like Pac-Man, simulations such as Football Manager 2020, to big-budget titles that include Global Offensive, Portal and Half-Life: Alyx.

There are numerous games that are free to play - Crusader Kings II and Ring of Elysium being just two examples.

For bargain hunters, Steam offers regular weekend and midweek sales with many games available at substantial reductions. If you really want to save money though, Steam also has seasonal sales with even bigger discounts on individual games, entire libraries from publishers, or select bundles of games.

For the community-minded, there is a Friends list for voice and text chat. There is also Clans, a feature that makes it possible to set up player groups who can take part in each other's games, and organise group activities.

To use Steam, you must create an account which can be shared with up to five others. Only one player can use the account at a time, though. Steam Family Share lets you lend your games to others.

OBS Studio

OBS Studio is a popular open-source application that lets you record your gameplay and stream it on platforms like Twitch and YouTube. It can also be used as a screen capture utility.

The program is feature-rich, which can make it difficult to get to grips with but, once you've mastered it, it's extremely useful for online gaming. A useful feature is a wizard that helps optimise your system for recording or streaming video.

While there are other programs, such as Plays and Nvidia's GeForce Experience, that do much the same as OBS Studio, there are some things none of them do as well. For example, if you want to record your gameplay and then create a YouTube tutorial, OBS Studio provides the ideal platform to do it.

To use OBS Studio, you first create a "Scene" where all your recording sources are kept. That done, you then add the sources - a game, your web-cam, microphone, watermark, etc. Once you're set up and ready to go, click the Start Recording button, fire up your game and start playing. When you're finished, click Stop Recording. The outputs from all the various sources will be merged into one output, which can then be streamed.

Not only can you record from a webcam and microphone, you can also incorporate footage from games, add videos and pictures, capture a window or section of your screen, and much more besides.

OBS Studio is used by professional gamers and broadcasters who appreciate its powerful features. The fact it's free is an added bonus.

GameSpot

GameSpot is a site that every gamer should add to their Favourites. Dedicated to gaming, it provides news, reviews, previews, downloads, deals, forums and blogs - just about everything you could expect from a gaming website, in fact.

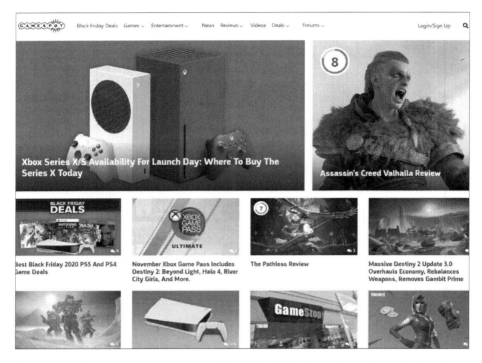

Gaming platforms covered include PC, PS4, PS5, Xbox One, Xbox Series X, Switch, Stadia and 3DS. The site provides you with literally thousands of articles about games, gaming hardware, manufacturers, events, etc.

The very popular Video section of the site offers trailers from over two thousand games. These give prospective buyers an insight into a game's visuals, storyline, hardware requirements, performance, load time and more, before parting with the cash.

Also useful are the site's forums. These cover every conceivable topic that are likely to be of interest to the gamer. Boards include game discussion, Nintendo, Play-Station and retro gaming, to name just a few. There are also boards dedicated to popular games, such as Minecraft and Final Fantasy.

GameSpot is not just about gaming either. Click the Entertainment tab and you will be able to catch up with the latest information on movies, television, Netflix, Star Wars and even, for some bizarre reason, wrestling.

Discord

Discord is an extremely popular chat application much used by gamers. It offers text, VoIP, and video chat servers, plus more specialised features for gamers, such as Twitch integration.

At its basic level, Discord enables users to message each other via servers, also known as communities. Each of these servers comprises text channels for communication via text messaging, and voice channels for chatting with other users. Each server has a number of channels, each of which is dedicated to a different topic or has different rules. For example, one channel might be used to talk about a specific game, with another being used for general chit-chat.

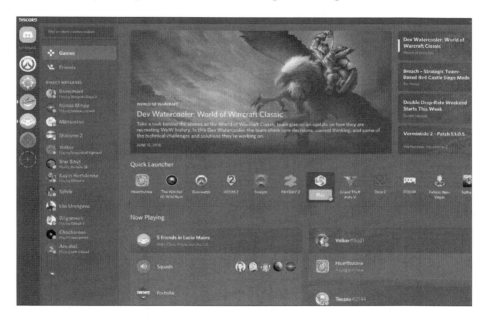

While there are thousands of Discord servers covering all sorts of subjects, the majority of them are dedicated to gaming. Indeed, serving the gaming community is what Discord was originally created to do. Seeing the potential it offers, other communities have joined in. Currently, around 250 million people use it, with the Fortnite server alone having some 500,000 members.

Discord can also be connected to other applications, such as Spotify and YouTube, which further adds to its functionality. Plus, with versions for PCs and mobile devices, it is more versatile than many of its competitors.

The basic application is free and will be perfectly adequate for most users. However, there is always the option to upgrade to Discord Nitro. For a fee, you get improved features that include higher resolution video, higher upload limits and better quality streaming.

Gamasutra

Gamasutra is a site devoted to all aspects of video game development. It won't be for everyone, but gamers who want to learn about their passion rather than just play all the time, will find it provides a lot of relevant info and resources.

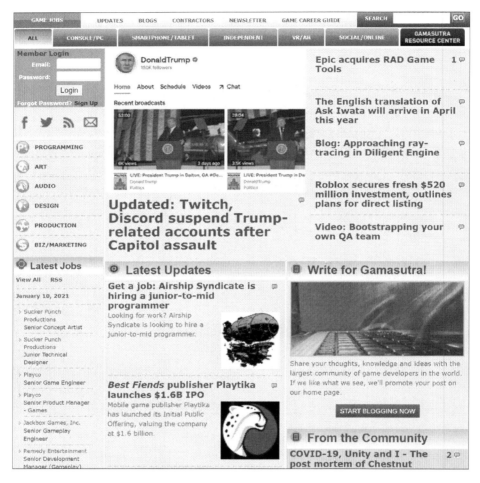

The site offers articles and news for all the gaming platforms - PCs, consoles, smartphones and tablets. These cover every aspect of game development, including programming, art, audio, video, design, production and marketing.

Resources include a jobs market place, guides to careers in the gaming industry, advertising, a newsletter, industry news and more.

There is also a thriving social community with blogs and forums. Those of you interested in what goes on behind the scenes, as it were, will find Gamasutra well worth a look.

Hamachi

Multi-player gaming has always been extremely popular and is becoming ever more so. Basically, it works by using a network to provide a common medium that players can connect their machines to.

Two types of network are used: local area networks (LAN) and virtual private networks (VPN). In the early days of the Internet, when it was painfully slow, LANs were the way to go. However, this type of network does have inherent drawbacks - bulky equipment to move around, connection issues, etc.

So, with the vast improvement in Internet speeds, playing games online via VPNs has largely taken over thanks to the sheer convenience they afford. With a few clicks of the mouse button, you can be playing against someone on the other side of the world within seconds.

This is where Hamachi comes in. It provides a platform for the creation and management of virtual networks that can be used for any number of purposes, of which gaming is the most popular.

As we all know, the Internet is fraught with dangers so a great feature of the platform is that it uses the AES-256-CBC cipher for data encryption and decryption. This makes its networks extremely secure. Other security features include password protection that prevents people joining a network without invitation, and membership approval.

Hamachi is easy to set up and use, and doesn't require an in-depth knowledge of VPNs and technical issues such as port forwarding, for example. This is one of the reasons it's so popular with online gamers. The free option allows a maximum of five people to connect to a network at a time.

UserBenchmark

We've mentioned benchmarking utilities several times in this book and here we're going to look at our favourite one of all - UserBenchmark. This program gives your PC an overall rating, plus individual ratings for the main components.

Open the utility and it will run a series of tests that evaluates all parts of your system, and then display the results in a browser window. The test takes about 10 to 15 minutes to complete, depending on the PC's speed.

The basic ratings are shown at the top of the page. If you scroll down, you will see them displayed in more detail. A very useful feature is the comparison chart that lets you see how your system stacks up against those of over 30 million other users.

Index

Printed in Great Britain
by Amazon

70773138R00099